IMAGES OF ENGLAND

STEVENAGE STREETS

IMAGES OF ENGLAND

STEVENAGE STREETS

MARGARET ASHBY

TEMPUS

Frontispiece: A maginificent fifteenth century crown post in the roof of the recently rediscovered Falcon Inn, Stevenage High Street.

OTHER BOOKS BY MARGARET ASHBY

The Book of Stevenage
The Book of the River Lea
Forster Country
Stevenage Past
A Hertfordshire Christmas
Stevenage, History and Guide
Stevenage Voices
Voices of Benslow Music Trust
St Nicholas' Church: Recent Research I (ed. Margaret Ashby)

First published 2004

Tempus Publishing Limited
The Mill, Brimscombe Port,
Stroud, Gloucestershire, GL5 2QG

© Margaret Ashby, 2004

The right of Margaret Ashby to be identified as the Author of this work has been asserted in accordance with the Copyrights, Designs and Patents Act 1988.

British Library Cataloguing in Publication Data.
A catalogue record for this book is available from the British Library.

ISBN 0 7524 3369 5

Typesetting and origination by Tempus Publishing Limited
Printed in Great Britain

Contents

Acknowledgements

When I agreed to write this book, I was mindful of the pioneering work of the late George Lack, whose booklet *Stevenage Street Names* was published by the Stevenage Society in 1967, and ran into several editions before his untimely death in 1984. Since then, not only have many more roads been built, but also much new research has been carried out into various aspects of Stevenage history. The Stevenage Society is currently planning to update Mr Lack's book.

I would also like to acknowledge the work of the late Joyce Lenton, whose *Stevenage Chronicle* is a masterly summary of the early and recent history of Stevenage. First written for schoolchildren, it was subsequently extended, updated and published by the Development Corporation in 1975. It provides an invaluable short cut to disentangling the complicated progress of developments that were taking place during the first thirty years of the New Town. Joyce, a graduate of Oxford University, was Assistant Social Relations Officer for the Development Corporation. She had previously worked in Fleet Street on two national newspapers, where she researched answers to queries and readers' letters. After retirement she won the Senior Citizen Brain of Britain award.

I am very grateful for the enormous amount of help I have been given by many people while I have been researching this book. The following, listed in alphabetical order, have been particularly generous in sharing their time, information or photographs:

John Amess; Ian and Patricia Aspinall; John Austin; Jean Baker; Alan Cudmore; Tony Evenden; Roy Findley; Betty Game; Adrian Gibson; Ray Gorbing; Margaret Haas; Hertfordshire Archives and Local Studies (HALS) staff; Don Hills; Steven Hodges; Stella Kestin; David Kissane; Anne and Aris Mariner; Stanley and Sybil Marriott; Wilfred Neilson; Brian Norman; Lorna and Ken Poole; John Richardson; Mary Spicer; Stevenage Library staff; Jean Trend; Stevenage Museum staff, especially Claire Hills; Annette Stewart, for the photographs of the Barclay family; David Stewart, for the photographs by Lt Col. Chalmers and Leslie Chalmers; Janet Walker and the late Mrs Linnaea Walker; Anne Sworder; Linda Young of Alta Image, Stevenage, and many others who have helped with information or in practical ways.

Introduction

Stevenage originated as a Saxon village although, increasingly, evidence is coming to light of previous Romano-British settlements. By 1086, when William the Conqueror's Domesday survey was made, the Saxons had a village named Stigenace, built on the hill where St Nicholas' church stands today. The centre of population subsequently shifted down to the road half-a-mile away. The move brought prosperity and during the Middle Ages, Stevenage developed into a market town. In 1281 the Abbot of Westminster, as Lord of the Manor, was granted a charter for a weekly market and annual fair. Stevenage High Street grew up on the main road from London to the north, which became known as the Great North Road and later as the A1. In the eighteenth and nineteenth centuries the town became well known to travellers and many of the old coaching inns still exist in the High Street.

In 1850 the railway came to Stevenage, with the opening of a station on the Great Northern line. The population increased steadily and Stevenage became in part a commuter town, being a convenient thirty miles from King's Cross. However, by 1900, with a population of 3,000, it was still very much a country town, dominated by agriculture and rural trades.

By the end of the Second World War, the population had risen to 6,200 and there was one sizeable factory and several small ones dispersed around the town, but in essentials it was unchanged. Then, in 1946, Stevenage was designated the first of a number of New Towns which were to be 'satellites' of London on a radius of approximately thirty miles from the capital, with the aim of providing homes for Londoners bombed out during the war. Under this legislation, the population would increase tenfold, to 60,000 people. As required by the government, a Master Plan for the development of the designated area was prepared in 1949, another in 1955 and a third in 1966, which controlled development until 1980, when the Development Corporation ceased to exist. Subsequent private developments have taken place and the population at present is nearly 80,000 people.

During the building of the New Town, a number of existing buildings were demolished and one or two roads were completely obliterated. Some other roads were re-routed, renamed or made almost unrecognisable. Inevitably, the most dramatic and visible change has been the loss of green space, as agricultural land has been built over. However, a very high percentage of the pre-1946 buildings and almost all the streets do remain, although their context has altered.

The street names of Stevenage generally fall into one of three groups:

1. Pre-New Town roads: These include a few ancient streets and lanes, records of which exist in medieval documents and roads built in the nineteenth and early twentieth centuries, named after fields, local features or personalities.

2. Early roads built by the Development Corporation: Most of their names are based on research into old documents and are based on field names, but they are not always in the correct location. Thus, while they keep the names alive, they can be confusing for anyone studying the history of the town. In this group may also be included roads named after prominent local people, but it was the Development Corporation's policy not to use famous names while the subject was still alive.

3. Later roads built either by the Development Corporation or by private developers, with names that have no relation to the history of their locality: These include the 'themed' roads, for example those in the Chells neighbourhood named after famous women and the seaside town names in Symonds Green. This idea arose because of a shortage of local names when several roads were built in one large field.

The New Town was designed as a group of neighbourhoods clustered around a new town centre and based on existing hamlets and farms. The neighbourhoods originally proposed were: Old Stevenage, Bedwell, Broadwater, Shephall, Chells and Pin Green. The village of Shephall, formerly a separate entity, was incorporated into the designated New Town area. Subsequently, Symonds Green was added as the seventh neighbourhood and in recent years there have been additional large private developments tacked on to the planned town.

In the early days of the Development Corporation, a Street Naming Committee was established, chaired by Councillor Philip Ireton, to decide procedures for naming the great number of new roads being built. The Committee included representatives from the Development Corporation, the Urban District Council, the Head Postmaster and the Fire Service, the latter to comment on any proposed name that might be confused with one already existing and thus possibly cause delay in answering emergency calls. The Committee's work resulted in a list of names approved for use in the various neighbourhoods and is essentially the system in use today, although it is open to developers and others to suggest names for approval by the Borough Council.

In compiling this book I have not, of course, been able to cover every existing road and building, but I have attempted to include roads from all parts of the town. Nor has it been possible to give an equal amount of space to every road or building name and I have

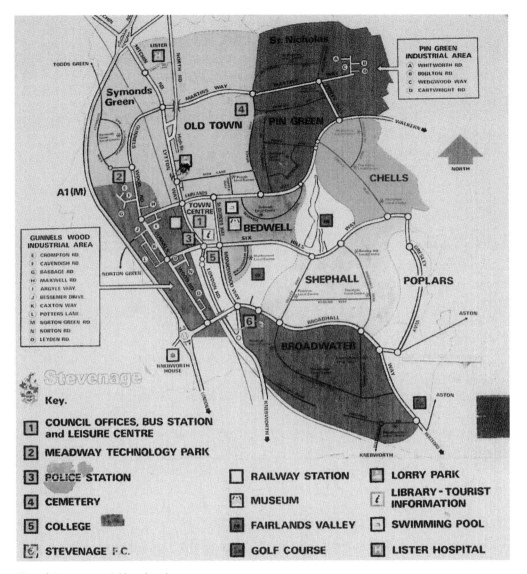

Plan of Stevenage neighbourhoods.

selected some for more detailed coverage on the basis of their known history or their prominent locations. I have also deliberately gone in some detail into the history of two old buildings owned by the Borough Council on behalf of the local community – Springfield House and Fairlands Farmhouse.

A NOTE ON LOCAL AUTHORITIES

From 1946, when Stevenage was designated a new town, there have been several changes of local authority names and powers. Rather than use abbreviations, which are confusingly similar, I have adopted the following usages throughout this book:

Urban District Council – Stevenage Urban District Council was established under the Local Government Act of 1894 to replace the former Local Board of Health.

Development Corporation – Stevenage Development Corporation was appointed by the Minister of Town and Country Planning, following the New Towns Act of 1946. It had responsibility for carrying out the development of Stevenage in accordance with a Master Plan and was dissolved on 30 September 1980, on completion of its work.

Borough Council – Stevenage Borough Council was established in 1974, as a result of the 1972 Local Government Act, to replace the Urban District Council.

Hertfordshire County Council – Came into existence in 1889, following the Local Government Act of 1888. Its responsibilities include (with some exceptions) education, health services, police, fire and ambulance services and highways within the county, including Stevenage.

Bibliography

PRIMARY SOURCES

Census Records for Stevenage (Stevenage Central Library and Hertfordshire Archives and Local Studies, Hertford (HALS)

Extent and Terrier of the Manor of Stevenage, 1315 and 1323, (Cambridge University Library KK5/29 ff78-83)

Fairlands Farm documents, various (HALS)

Hall, Revd H., *Names of places in Hertfordshire, a paper,* (St Albans Archaeological & Architectural Society, 17 June 1858)

Jeremiah Inns, Will and papers relating to Springfield House (Stevenage Borough Council)

Seager, Mary, *Diary* (privately owned)

Stevenage Almshouse Records (Stevenage Borough Council and HALS)

Stevenage Development Corporation archive (HALS)

Stevenage Urban District Council Minutes (Stevenage Museum)

Whitney Wood and Barclay family documents (HALS)

SECONDARY SOURCES

Amess, John, *Call out the Engine,* Stevenage Society, 1997

Balchin, Jack, *First New Town,* Stevenage Development Corporation, 1980

Chauncy, Sir Henry, *History and Antiquities of the County of Hertfordshire,* 1700, reprinted by Kohler & Coombes, Dorking, 1975

Going, C.J. and Hunn, *Jonathan, Excavations at Boxfield Farm, Chells, Stevenage, Hertfordshire,* Hertfordshire Archaeological Trust, Report No. 2, 1999

de Salis, Dorothy & Stephens, Richard, *An Innings Well Played,* Alleyne's Old Boys Association, 1989

Domesday Book; Hertfordshire, trans. John Morris, Phillimore, 1976

Gover, J.E.B. *et.al., The Place Names of Hertfordshire,* English Place Names Society, 1995

Johnson, W. Branch, *The Little Guide to Hertfordshire,* 5e, Methuen & Co., 1957

Jolliffe, Graham & Jones, Arthur, *Hertfordshire Inns and Public Houses,* Hertfordshire Publications, 1995

Lenton, Joyce, *A Stevenage Chronicle,* Stevenage Development Corporation, 1975

Methold, E.V. *Notes on Stevenage,* St Albans, 1902

Moore, Cyril, *Hertfordshire Windmills and Windmillers,* Windsup Publications, 1999

New Town of Stevenage, Stevenage Development Corporation, 1949

Novak, Bernard, *Thorns and roses; a chronicle of hope,* Able Publishing, 1993

Page, W. ed. *The Victoria County History of Hertfordshire, vol. 12,* 1912, reprinted by the University of London Institute of Historical Research, 1971

Pitcher, June, *Sketch map of Stevenage in 1836,* Stevenage Society, 2e. 1980

Spicer, C.M. *Tyme out of mind,* 1984

Trow-Smith, Robert, *History of Stevenage,* Stevenage Society 1958 and 2nd ed. at www.stevenage.gov.uk/the town/history

Young, Arthur, *General View of the Agriculture of Hertfordshire,* 1804, David & Charles Reprints, 1971

CHAPTER ONE

Primary Roads

The Great North Road

Roads have shaped Stevenage's history from its earliest days, when the main population of Saxon Stigenace moved down to the point we now call the Bowling Green, where the major north-south road divided to become today's Hitchin Road and North Road. The latter had existed before the Romans arrived in this country, but they straightened and widened it and used it as one of their main transport arteries. In about AD 100, wealthy local Romano-British families built the Six Hills burial mounds beside the Roman Road where they have intrigued travellers ever since. For many centuries, this was a lonely stretch of road and the Six Hills were visible from a considerable distance.

As the Roman age was forgotten, stories abounded about the origin of the Six Hills.

Six Hills, beside the Great North Road.

Stevenage district, 6" Ordnance Survey map, 1946 edition.

One popular myth told of the Devil digging in Whomerley Wood (see Chapter Five) and throwing shovels full of earth over his shoulder where they landed in six heaps beside the road. In the nineteenth century they were believed to be of Danish origin. Today, surrounded by modern buildings, with the traffic on the B197 sweeping past on their eastern side and the remains of the old Great North Road reduced to a cycle track on the west, they seem less imposing, but they remain monuments of the greatest historic importance to Stevenage.

At Broadwater, where it was joined by another ancient road from Hertford, the Roman road continued, albeit with many twists and turns, to London. Over the centuries it became so heavily used and its maintenance so neglected that, in common with most other roads at the time, turnpike trusts were established to improve it. This was done in sections. The Stevenage and Biggleswade Trust was set up in 1720 to look after the thirteen miles from Stevenage to Biggleswade and, from 1726, a separate trust dealt with the section from Stevenage through Hatfield to Lemsford Mill. Then, in 1757, The Watton Trust was established to improve the road from Hertford to Broadwater.

The turnpike roads did not make great profits for their investors – many lost money – but they did create the means for swifter and more convenient travel. The era of stage-coaches, post-chaises and mail coaches brought prosperity to Stevenage and the many old inns still remaining in today's High Street bear witness to the number of travellers who refreshed themselves with food and drink here. There was a tollgate at the Coach and Horses, formerly called the New Inn, and another known as the Stevenage Turnpike, in North Road, conveniently near the Marquess of Granby alehouse. Turnpike Close, a house-name in Rectory Lane nearby, keeps alive the memory of those days. The Swan Inn on the Bowling Green was the biggest and most superior of the inns. It was fortunate in having a succession of excellent innkeepers, including Richard Bowcocke, or Brecocke, mentioned in Samuel Pepys' diary for 1667 as 'the best host I know almost'. The Rockingham coach was one of several that stopped at the White Lion, where passengers had to dismount on rough ground at the side of the building because the archway into the inn yard was too low for a laden coach to pass through. Of the other coaching inns, the Red Lion and the White Hart are still flourishing in the High Street, but others have become business premises or private houses. The latest to close its doors was the Yorkshire Grey, sometimes known as the White Horse, where once the trustees of the Stevenage and Biggleswade Turnpike Trust used to hold meetings, which has in the last year become an Italian restaurant.

The White Lion, early twentieth century.

London Road

From Sish Lane to Broadwater, the Great North Road was known as London Road. However, the arrival of Fairlands Way cut it in two, creating a dead end until a footbridge was erected in 1971. The cedar trees below the footbridge stood in the garden of the Firs, a large house owned in the early twentieth century by the Walpole family. There is a memorial tablet in Holy Trinity church to Horatio Spencer Walpole, Lieutenant of the Coldstream Guards, who was killed in action in the First World War, in the trenches near Arras on 9 April 1918, aged thirty-six. Later the house became the Home Hospital for Women until 1973, when it was closed and used by the Urban District Council as temporary accommodation for young families with urgent housing needs. Its entrance was in Ditchmore Lane, the name of which has now been used for the remaining stretch of London Road in the Old Town.

Stevenage was very proud of its position on the foremost road in the country, with the name 'Great North Road' and the later designation A1, when the system of numbering roads in a clockwise circle based on London was introduced. Of course, it was this very road, together with the Great Northern Railway, which made Stevenage, thirty miles from London, ideally suited to become Britain's first post-war New Town following the 1946 New Towns Act. From that time, new primary roads were built, shaping the landscape of a new urban Stevenage and helping to define each of the neighbourhoods. An essential part

The Firs, later Home Hospital for Women, London Road.

The Queen inspecting rockets at the English Electric factory during a visit to Stevenage, 1959.

of the plan was the building of a bypass for through traffic. This was the responsibility of the County Council acting on the instructions of the Ministry of Transport. Work did not begin until 1960 and the road was finally opened as the A1 (M) in 1962. Although it did not have the romantic history of the old road, its arrival brought relief to the High Street, clogged with constant traffic day and night.

Before the bypass was completed, the Development Corporation had built several new primary roads, which were already in use. An important concept of New Town planning was the separation of industry from residential areas and Gunnells Wood Road was designed as the major access road to the employment area in the west of the town. Built in sections beginning in 1963, it runs parallel to the A1 (M) and lies between it and the railway line, linking with Martin's Way to the north and Broadhall Way to the south. The name Gunnells Wood is taken from a small wood at the extreme southwest of Stevenage, near the boundary with Knebworth. It is a name of Scandinavian origin and probably means 'Gunnhilda's Wood'. There was also a house called 'Gunnells' or 'Gunnell's Park' built in New Road (now called Fairview Road) in about 1906 for John Inns, by the long-established Stevenage firm of W. Austin.

Fairlands

Fairlands Way, built between 1952 and 1970, links the Industrial Area on the west of Stevenage to Gresley Way. The eastern section of Fairlands Way, from just south of Douglas Drive, follows the line of the old road from Stevenage to Walkern. It takes its name from Fairlands Farm, and its fields have since become Fairlands Valley Park. The name 'Fairlands' is also Scandinavian in origin, as explained by the Revd H. Hall in 1858, '"Faircraft" and "Fairland" are derived, not from our adjective "fair" but from the Scandinavian "faar", the sheep...' The spelling of Fairlands has varied over the centuries. It was sometimes referred to as 'Fair Lane' or 'Fairlawn'.

By 1684 the farm was owned by Sir William Lytton of Knebworth, and then consisted of 369 acres of land. In that year the tenant farmer, William Titmouse, or Tyttmus, died and the lease was transferred to his widow Rebecca and his son William for a rent of £100 per year. A copy of the inventory of 'all and singular the goods, chattells and creditts of William Tyttmus of Fairlands' has survived, signed by Samuel Hodgson, Thomas Harvy and John Clisbe and dated 28 January 1685, The total valuation was £815 19d 08s.

It is possible to trace some of the nineteenth century tenants from the census returns. In 1841 John and Jemima French were farming at 'Fairland'. Ten years later, their children, Henry French and his sister Mary, were still at Fairland and the record shows that they farmed 400 acres. By 1861 only Mary was left, but she was still farming, with nine men and four boys in her employment. The farm was then listed as 'Fairlawn'. In 1871, William and Mary Ann Titmus, who were employing twelve men and five boys, were farming the 359 acres at 'Fairland'. For about thirty years, from 1881, when they were farming 350 acres with a staff of six men and six boys, William and Anne Roberts were at Fairlands. Rupert Marriott followed them and was succeeded by his son, Stanley who, with his wife Sybil, was the last to farm at Fairlands.

In their 1949 publication, *The New Town of Stevenage,* the Development Corporation stated, 'Fairlands Valley, which runs from north to south through the middle of the site, will remain open space' and its original intention was for farming to continue there. The farm at that time was owned by Gonville and Caius College, Cambridge, as was much other land in Stevenage. The Development Corporation served a compulsory purchase order on it in 1951, but allowed the farmer to remain as tenant until 1968. In the 1966 Master Plan, the proposal was for Fairlands Valley to become the town's principal area of recreation, with artificially created lakes as well as green space. Consequently the land was transferred to the Urban District Council who carried out the work with initial financial support from the Development Corporation.

The southern section of Fairlands Valley was opened to the public in 1970 and engineering and landscaping work by Stevenage Urban District Council began on the northern section, including the lakes. But the 1966 Master Plan also included proposals to build a new road – known as Road 9 – through Fairlands Valley from Broadhall Way. A protest group, the Stevenage Valley Association, was set up to oppose the building of

Fairlands Farmhouse.

Fairlands Farm, sale of last herd of cattle, 1957.

Road 9. A petition of over 12,000 signatures at first made no impact, but was eventually successful and plans for Road 9 were dropped. In 1972 Fairlands Valley Park was opened by Sir Alec Rose for the Urban District Council, to cater for various leisure pursuits with emphasis on water sports.

In 1995, in recognition of their help, Bedwell School in Telford Avenue, which overlooks Fairlands, was renamed Marriotts School in honour of Stanley and Sybil Marriott. Since 1990 Stevenage Borough Council has made Fairlands Farmhouse available to The Digswell Arts Trust.

Six Hills

Six Hills Way, begun in 1953, to link Gunnels Wood Road with Shephall Way and Chells Way, has since been extended to Gresley Way. It must be emphasized here that, although named after the Six Hills, this is an entirely modern road of the mid-twentieth century which runs at right angles across the line of the ancient Six Hills beside London Road. As it passes the town centre, it overlooks the Asda supermarket on the site of the Stevenage Further Education College which was opened here in 1961. The new North Herts. College was built on the playing fields and opened by Her Majesty Queen Elizabeth II in March 2003.

Previously, for nearly fifty years, this site had been the famous Six Hills Nursery, opened by Clarence Elliott in 1907. Specialising in alpine plants, the nursery attracted eminent clients, including the Duchess of Gloucester and members of the Bowes Lyon family of St Paul's, Waldenbury. Many plants propagated at Six Hills had local names, such as the gentian *Stevenagensis* and the primula *Barbara Barker*, named after the daughter of Frank Barker, manager of the nursery. The fuchsia named after Mrs Popple was found by Clarence Elliott growing in his neighbour's garden at 41 London Road. This was one of several large houses, mostly built in the late nineteenth century and which E.M. Forster described in *Howard's End* as 'the ugly new houses built down the London Road', all of which were demolished to make way for the New Town centre.

Nearby was the Guild of Literature and Arts, the well-intentioned brainchild of Charles Dickens and Sir Edward Bulwer Lytton, over which they expended much time and energy. Dickens first came to Knebworth House in 1850 and it was then that the idea was born. The following extracts from the Dickens Centenary Exhibition at Knebworth House tell the story: 'Bulwer Lytton would present the Guild with the use of a plot of land on his estate, where a group of neat cottages would be built and in them would dwell, rent-free, a little fellowship of artists and men of letters...Over them would preside a warden'. In 1865, the splendid Gothic building comprising three guild houses was completed in London Road, just north of the Six Hills. Dickens arrived by train for the dedication, the culmination of years of fundraising. Unfortunately, the scheme was not successful. It proved difficult to find suitable applicants; for example one man preferred to pay rent for

Above: Mrs Popple fuchsia.

Right: 1881 Ordnance Survey map, 25″ to the mile, showing Guild of Arts and Literature.

accommodation in Bedford so that his sons could attend the Bedford Foundation School and another refused to be 'buried alive' in Stevenage. In 1897 the guild houses were sold and the proceeds shared between the Royal Literary Fund and the Artists' General Benevolent Fund. The building was demolished in 1960.

Almost opposite the guild houses, on the other side of London Road, was Our Mutual Friend, the public house named to celebrate the publication of Dickens' novel of the same name. It was served with a compulsory purchase order by the Development Corporation, after which it was occupied for a time by the British Railways Staff Association before being pulled down in the early 1960s. The licence was transferred to the newly built public house in Broadwater Crescent, which perpetuates the name.

Stevenage also featured in one of Dickens' short stories in his annual *Christmas Stories* for 1861. In *Tom Tiddler's Ground*, he describes the High Street as 'wide for its height, silent for its size and drowsy in the dullest degree...[where] a score of weak little lath-and-plaster cabins clung in confusion about the Attorney's red-brick house.' It seems probable that he was sitting in the White Hart, when he made these observations. He was on his way to Redcoats Green, just outside Stevenage, to visit the hermit James Lucas, which was a fashionable thing to do at the time. His story describes that unfortunate man incarcerated by his own wish in a house that was decaying around him. The modern Tom Tiddler public house at Symonds Green takes its name from Dickens' story.

Broadhall Way, the A602, takes traffic from the A1 (M) to Hertford, replacing the old Hertford Road, which formerly joined the Great North Road at the Broadwater. The first section was built in 1956 and the name is made up from the first syllable of Broadwater and the second of Shephall, the two planned neighbourhoods which it divides, cutting through the ancient parish of Shephall.

At the Monkswood Way end is the roundabout for the aborted Road 9 and a car park for the southern entrance to Fairlands Valley, with pedestrian access to Monks Wood and Whomerley Wood. Opposite and accessible by underpass, is the ground of the Stevenage Borough Football Club, opened in 1961. The original Stevenage Football Ground had been sited between the Great North Road and the railway line, west of the Town Centre and near the new railway station, but was required for development under the 1966 master plan. Further along Broadhall Way, on ground that was previously part of Shephall Manor estate is the Shephalbury Sports Academy, a joint venture between the borough council, Stevenage Football Club and North Herts. College. At this point, Broadhall Way sweeps over the old Shephall Green Lane, which is now an underpass between Shephall village green and Shephalbury Park.

At the southern end of Broadhall Way, just beyond its junction with Shephall Way, is the running track at Ridlin's Wood, which was originally in the parish of Shephall and is mentioned in the 1840 tithe award. Stevenage Municipal Golf Course, on land formerly part of the grounds of Aston House, opened in 1980 near Bragbury End, which had previously been in Datchworth parish. The name Bragbury End probably means 'Hill marked by a clump of fern or brushwood'. In a document of 1294 it was given as 'Brakeburne' but over the years the spelling has varied, including 'Bragbury Grene' in 1429, 'Bragberg End' in 1598 and 'Brackberre End' in 1638.

Gresley Way is named after the engineer and locomotive designer Sir Nigel Gresley. Following the enlargement of Stevenage by the development of Chells Manor Village and the Poplars, Gresley Way was extended close to the new borough boundary, to connect Broadhall Way, Six Hills Way, Fairlands Way, and Martin's Way.

Martin's Way takes its name from Martin's Wood at the extreme east of the borough. Ordnance Survey maps show that the whole area centred on Box Wood, in Walkern parish, was heavily wooded in the nineteenth century. Martin's Wood and Wellfield Wood just to the north were probably once part of a continuous tract of woodland. Martin's Way passes the Pin Green industrial area where roads are named after famous engineers, none of whom have any connection with Stevenage history, but whose names reinforce the association with industry. Continuing through Pin Green to Canterbury Way, Martin's Way then enters the Old Town of Stevenage, where its passage disturbed the ancient landscape around St Nicholas' church and cut through the historic Avenue where in 1935 it had been planted with trees to commemorate the Silver Jubilee of King George V and Queen Mary, with money subscribed by local residents.

St Nicholas' church before the building of Martin's Way.

Martin's Way, with Avenue bridge in the distance.

CHAPTER TWO

HIGH STREET

Medieval Buildings

In 1281, the Abbot of Westminster was granted a charter to hold a fair and a market in his manor of Stevenage. Since then the High Street has developed over the centuries as the centre of commercial life in Stevenage. Known as Fore Street until the mid-nineteenth century, it grew piecemeal from the road fork at the north end, gradually extending down towards Sish Lane, at which point it changed its name to London Road. It continued on through quiet fields and empty spaces, past the Six Hills standing in splendid isolation and the sometimes flooded road at Broadwater, on its way to London.

More old buildings remain on the west (even numbered) side of the High Street than on the east where many were burned down in the fires of 1807 and 1829. Most of the oldest in today's High Street are near the Bowling Green, although many have been altered and modernised, often more than once, and now present deceptive fronts to the world. One such is number 28, currently Hamilton Davies Solicitors. The large plate glass windows, probably put in at the beginning of the twentieth century, give no indication of the true age of the building, which dates from the medieval period.

Springfield House

Springfield House, number 24, is not one of the oldest High Street buildings but it has an interesting history, closely connected with a variety of individuals who have made an impact on the history of Stevenage. It must not be confused with Springfield Passage and Springfield Cottage, [see below] although it is not impossible that in the distant past there was a connection. Surviving records show that Springfield House was owned from about 1850 by the Triphook family, through whom it descended to Charlotte Aldham. At this time surprising changes were taking place in the High Street. The town's chief coaching inn, the Swan, its trade having been drastically reduced by the coming of the railway in 1850, was closed. Concurrently, Alleyne's Grammar School, almost next door, was also having problems. A master was being sought to replace the elderly incumbent who was

Above: Bowling Green, early twentieth century.

Left: Medieval window and jetty at number 28 High Street.

long overdue for retirement. The new arrival was the Reverend John Osborne Seager who arrived not long before the Swan was put on the market. In 1850 he bought it, changed its name to the Grange and set up a private school there. It very quickly established itself as a highly regarded preparatory school and Seager's fortunes flourished so well that he was able to buy Springfield House in 1884. The precise details of the move are known because Seager's daughter, Mary, kept a diary, in which she recorded:

Grange School grounds, 1910.

11th January 1884 – Moved to Springfield.
14th January 1884 – New Library at Springfield roofed in.
12th May 1884 – Father completed the purchase of Springfield from Miss Aldham.

Charlotte Aldham, from whom the Seager's bought Springfield, was recorded in the 1841 census as holding the office of Postmistress. It is likely that she had not lived at Springfield for some time, as the 1871 census shows that the house was then occupied by a Mr Collins, but owned by Charlotte Aldham. However, it is clear that she was not far away and also that she was on very good terms with the Seagers. An entry in Mary Seager's diary for 1886 records, '17th February – Miss Aldham very ill, alone with Miss Triphook, fetched to Springfield,' and on 19 February, 'Miss Aldham died in her old bedroom'.

John Osborne Seager died on 4 April 1889. His son, John Lingen Seager, having succeeded him at the Grange School, moved away by 1919 and sold Springfield to a Mr Parker for £1,600. The next phase of the saga began in 1922, when Jeremiah Inns bought the house. He was a remarkable man, the son of an even more remarkable father, the self-made millionaire John Inns.

In 1935 Mary (née Ellis) wife of Jeremiah Inns, died, and in 1936 he married again, Helen Cadzow Walker. He appears to have given his wife a free hand to effect the total refurbishment of Springfield House. For the next two years she devoted herself to obtaining materials and fitments of the highest quality, mostly from leading London

Springfield House.

furnishers, to make Springfield House into an elegant and modern home. Her attention to detail was impressive and she kept all the catalogues, patterns and quotations for further reference. While she was doing this, the famous Adelphi Terrace in the Strand, built by the Adams brothers, was demolished and the furniture and fittings sold. Helen Inns bought a number of items, including doors, for Springfield House.

Throughout the Second World War, Helen Inns worked hard to support the war effort. She is particularly associated with the Women's Royal Voluntary Service forces canteen, which she set up at the Old Castle Inn (now NatWest Bank) in Middle Row. This provided food and drink and a place to relax for service men billeted in the town, or soldiers passing through. It was recognised as one of the best of its kind in the country. She also invited Home Guard troops and service men to Springfield House and held garden parties and other fundraising social events.

In 1945, Jeremiah Inns died, leaving Springfield House to his wife for her lifetime, after which it was to go to the Stevenage Urban District Council for use as a Cottage Hospital. Helen Inns lived until 1968, by which time life had changed. The country had a National Health Service which was about to build a new hospital at Stevenage to serve the whole of north Hertfordshire. Small cottage hospitals were no longer needed. Discussions and legal wrangles about the future of Springfield House went on for several years until in 1971 it came into the ownership of the Development Corporation, under the New Towns Act regulations which allowed house owners within the designated area to require the

Corporation to buy their property. It subsequently became the Old Town Community Centre, also housing the Denington Gallery for the Stevenage Artists' Co-operative, and has been much appreciated by Old Town residents. Unfortunately, in 1976 Lytton Way cut through its large and beautiful garden and what was left was further divided by the road, with one piece made into a tiny park between Lytton Way and Orchard Crescent.

Jeremiah Inns left the town other legacies, including Inns Close old people's bungalows, in Letchmore Road. It is also possible to see his 'signature' on buildings including the 'new' post office built in 1913 opposite Springfield House.

The Cromwell

Further down the High Street, the Cromwell is so called because the house is believed to have been owned by John Thurloe, Secretary of State to Oliver Cromwell from 1652-1660, but despite efforts by several researchers, no documentary evidence of this has so far been found. The property originally was a farm probably stretching back to Church Lane, its fields covering what are now Basil's Road, Walkern Road and Stanmore Road. It may well have been acquired by Thurloe as one of several that he owned during Cromwell's rule, but even if this were so, it does not necessarily mean that he ever lived there. It is known that Cromwellian soldiers passed through Stevenage during the Civil War and no doubt on occasion some of them, perhaps even Cromwell himself, lodged in the town. A farmhouse in the main road would have been a very suitable place for rest and refreshment, particularly if in the hands of a trusted civil servant such as Thurloe. But this is all mere speculation.

A tithe list in the Hertfordshire County Record Office records that the property, including a cottage, barn, stables and garden, was owned in 1770 by William and Martha Oakley. A record of 1837 indicates that the property at that time consisted of half-an-acre of pasture, together with garden and the house. The building dates from the seventeenth century, but there has been considerable refurbishment throughout. It was enlarged in the early twentieth century, at about the same time that the property next door, number 27, became the Central Temperance Hotel.

An interesting feature over the fireplace in the board room is a carved stone panel with the dates 1667 and the letters 'T' above 'H' and 'F'. Many suggestions, some facetious, have been made as to what they represent, but the most likely explanation is that the 'T' represents a surname and the 'H' and 'F' Christian names of husband and wife, or possibly two brothers. It is also probable that the stone, which is very heavy and deeply carved, may have been originally intended for display on the outside of a building, (not necessarily this one) and that it was placed here sometime later, perhaps when the building was being renovated.

John Thurloe had become the owner of a number of landed estates during his successful career as Cromwell's 'spymaster', but after the restoration to the English throne of King

Cromwell Hotel in
the 1970s.

Charles II, he was stripped of his power and wealth. He reverted to making his living as a
lawyer and died, aged fifty-one, in his chambers in Lincoln's Inn, on 21 February 1667.

During the first half of the twentieth century, the Cromwell Hotel, which had acquired
a licence for alcohol in 1929, became well known to discerning travellers on the Great
North Road. Its garden, fronting the High Street, was designed and planted by Clarence
Elliott's Six Hills Nursery staff with a most attractive rockery and stream.

During the Second World War Sir Henry Wood, founder of the BBC Promenade
Concerts, stayed at the Cromwell, presumably travelling by train to London to his work in
the world of music. In 1944 he was taken ill and was attended by his friend and near
neighbour, Dr B. Lyndon Skeggs, who lived a little further up the High Street, at number
11, and carried on his medical practice from there. On his instructions, Sir Henry Wood
was taken to the Hitchin Hospital, where he died.

In the second half of the twentieth century, the Cromwell Hotel was enlarged by the
acquisition of number 27, a building which had for some years been leased by its owner to
the Hertfordshire County Council for a mother and baby clinic and school dentist on the
ground floor, and a district nurse's flat on the first floor.

In the early 1970s Walkern Road was widened by demolishing half of the Cromwell
gardens, and, for a time, there was considerable anxiety about the future of the Cromwell
Cottages, also known as Providence Row, numbers 2-10 Walkern Road. They were given

Former surgery of Dr Skeggs, number 11 High Street. On the right is the 'new' post office built in 1913.

Pond in Walkern Road.

a Grade II listing in 1976, after plans to pull them down were averted and in 1979 there were abortive plans to transform them into luxury accommodation for the hotel manager. They are attractive today, although their windows to the street are shuttered and the doorways blocked up, but 100 years ago each one housed a large family, whose children spilled out onto a dusty road and played around the pond opposite. The latter has been filled in and a small cul-de-sac behind it given the name Pond Close.

High Street, former market place. Far left is the Central Temperance Hotel.

Middle Row

Stevenage Market never achieved the importance of that at Hitchin, and had to be revived by Royal Charter in 1694, but as a town on the main road from London to the north, it did acquire a reputation in the eighteenth century as a great cattle market. There were ponds in and near the High Street where cattle on their way to London could drink and fields behind the White Lion, opposite the market place, where they could be rested overnight. A market cross stood in the market place, near the Old Castle Inn and close to it was the Market Cross House, a name which still appeared in records in the late nineteenth century. The Old Castle Inn became a tourist attraction as the place where the coffin of grocer and publican, Henry Trigg, who died in 1724, could be seen resting on the rafters of a barn at the rear of the building. It is still there today, but empty of bones. At the request of the Nat West Bank, the owners of the property, it was taken down and repaired by Austins the undertakers in 1999.

Middle Row is thought to have originated in the middle ages when temporary market booths and stalls gradually became established as permanent dwellings. Most of the buildings here survived the great fire of 1807 although some were damaged. Number 11, currently used as the Oxfam charity shop, is a striking building with a mansard roof. It may have been built in two phases, with the brickwork dating to the late seventeenth century and the roof possibly replaced later. Its doorway to Baker Street is considered a fine example of early nineteenth century classical revival style. This building was the Bakers' Arms public house, until it closed in the 1920s, from which the name Baker Street is derived, but very little is known about its early history.

Above: Middle Row.

Opposite: Number 63 High Street, once the town's post office, later Chambers' Library.

On the opposite corner of Baker Street, number 9 Middle Row, is another interesting building, dating from the seventeenth century or earlier. It acquired its name in the late nineteenth or early twentieth century when it was bought by a Mr Buckingham, who may have been inspired by the memory of the coffee tavern called the Windsor Castle which had previously stood at number 69.

Post Offices

Number 63 High Street was, in the nineteenth century, Stevenage's first post office. An unfortunate occurrence made headlines in 1882 when the postmaster, Thomas Smith, was taken to court for embezzlement. In spite of a petition from many supporters who testified to his previous good character, he was sentenced to twelve months' imprisonment. Number 63 later became a stationer's and newsagent, known for much of the twentieth century as Chambers' Library

In 1887 a purpose-built post office was opened at number 52 High Street with furniture and fittings from the Educational Supply Association. During the building of the F.W. Woolworth store in 1939 this was one of the buildings which were demolished and the numbering of this part of the High Street changed, making for some confusion for those trying to work out today exactly where a particular business used to be.

The town's third post office, built by Jeremiah Inns in 1913 at number 13 High Street, closed in 1994 and moved into the Waitrose store at number 74a. This building, now much altered, had been for nearly 100 years a drapery and household goods store, owned, from the 1870s to about 1910, by J. Green, then briefly by S.G. Muncey, and from the 1930s to the 1960s by Henderson's, drapers, furniture and outfitters. Green Street, the road between numbers 74 and 76 High Street, and named after the draper, was chopped in half by the building of Lytton Way. The High Street end was then given the new name of Drapers' Way.

Left: A.G. Lines' ironmongery shop.

Opposite: The old Falcon Inn and Lloyd's chemist shop.

An Ironmongery lost and a Falcon found

Yet another change is occurring now to the familiar face of the High Street: number 76, for over 100 years an ironmongery and hardware store, is about to become a licensed restaurant. In 1885 J. Silk opened his ironmongery business here and subsequently enlarged and improved the building. Albert George Lines, whose previous premises were at numbers 128 and 130 High Street, bought it in 1922 and was joined by his son, Albert Ivory Lines. In 1965, they also took over number 78, previously Elsie Smith's Ladies' Outfitters. By this time, Albert Ivory Lines' own sons, Ian and Alan, had joined the family firm and in 1976 they reorganised the premises to create a modern self-service store. In 2004, having decided to retire, they closed the shop for the last time on 18 June, and Stevenage High Street is now poised for a new era.

Next door to number 76, the Red Lion has a recorded history dating back to 1676. There was also, very close to it, the Falcon, for which many references have survived until about 1800, when it seemed to disappear without trace. Then, miraculously, it was rediscovered, neglected and dilapidated, behind locked gates next to Lloyd's chemist at number 84 High Street.

Kevin O'Neill, who made the discovery, spent several years renovating it and in the process uncovered much of the original timber-framed building, including a crown post roof and the remains of a gallery which once overlooked the inn yard. In 2003, the Falcon was once more opened to the public.

A document in the Hertfordshire Archives and Local Studies, dated 1460, begins:

> Know, present and future people that I, John Toby of Stevenage demise, enfeoff and by this
> my present charter do confirm to Thomas Parker, chaplain, all those messuages, lands and
> tenements, with their appurtenances, called the Falcon, on the hope situate and lying in
> Stevenage aforesaid...

This document was in Latin, apart from the words 'on the hope' which were written in English, perhaps because there was no Latin equivalent. The word 'hope' here probably derives from an old English word meaning 'a piece of enclosed land in the midst of waste land' which gives an interesting picture on this part of the High Street in the early fifteenth century. It also confirms the Falcon as the oldest licensed building in the High Street, although at the time of writing it is about to become the Maharajah Indian Restaurant.

The Old Workhouse

The south end of the High Street was manorial waste, that is, uncultivated ground used for a variety of purposes. The Stevenage waste contained a pond, the town lock-up or cage where wrong-doers were temporarily incarcerated, and from about 1550, the timber-framed building now known as Tudor House, number 2 Letchmore Road. It was sold to the Stevenage Vestry and used as the parish workhouse from 1773 to 1835, after which it became a straw-plait school.

In 1855 the old workhouse was rented by Stevenage Gas and Coke Company for offices and to provide accommodation for its manager. Two large gasholders were built in the grounds, on the Sish Lane side. In 1958, trustees of the Stevenage Consolidated Charities agreed to sell the house to Eric Moore, who had lived there since 1934 as manager for the Stevenage Gas and Coke Company and its successor, the Eastern Gas Board. It has been carefully renovated in recent years and is currently occupied by the Archer Architectural Partnership.

Two Churches

In 1861, the pond in front of the old workhouse was filled-in and the church of the Holy Trinity built on the site, from designs by a young architect named Arthur Blomfield, nephew of the Stevenage Rector, Canon George Becher Blomfield and son of the Bishop of London who, as lord of the manor of Stevenage, had given the land. The opening of the new church was a great relief to parishioners living at the rapidly-expanding south end of the town, who were becoming weary of the long walk up to the parish church of St Nicholas, often to find when they arrived that there was standing room only. However, the new building almost immediately proved too small and fundraising for an extension was put in hand. This was achieved in stages and by 1884 a new nave and south door had been completed, but the new chancel was yet to be built. Dr Andrew Whyte Barclay of Whitney Wood (see Chapter Three) had been a generous supporter of the new church building and, following his sudden death in 1885, his widow undertook to complete the work and to erect a stained glass east window in his memory.

At 3 p.m. on Monday 30 November 1885, being St Andrew's Day, the Bishop of St Albans, with many local clergy, consecrated the new chancel of Holy Trinity designed by architects Tate and Popplewell and built by the local firm of Bates and Warren. The east window, designed and executed by Heaton, Butler and Baynes of London, has as its main subject 'The Ascension of Our Lord' with five small panels depicting 'The calling of Andrew', 'The loaves and fishes', 'Christ, Physician and Healer', 'The Raising of Jairus' Daughter' and 'The Miraculous Draught of Fishes'.

For many years the Stevenage straw plait market operated outdoors, in the space between Holy Trinity church, Southend Farm (known previously as Trinity Farm and before that, as the Wheatsheaves) and the High Street. When the town hall was built in Railway Street (later called Orchard Road), the straw plait market moved there.

The building of Holy Trinity church led to the redevelopment of an old road on the other side of the High Street, opposite Sish Lane. This was known as Brickkiln End until the arrival of the railway in 1850 had cut off the old brickfield from the town, although a level crossing was provided. The western part of the road has become the modern

Holy Trinity church showing chancel and Barclay memorial window, early twentieth century.

Brickkiln Road. On the east, or High Street side, new houses were built and the road was re-named Trinity Road, but there remained a row of seventeenth-century cottages, including the Lord Roberts and the White Swan beer houses. The latter became Gates' slaughterhouse. There was also a windmill here, from 1850 or earlier, which appears to have been burnt down in the 1890s. Between the old cottages on the south side of Trinity Road, a narrow passageway ran parallel to the London Road. This was Springfield Passage, a row of tiny dwellings which yet managed to accommodate whole families, whose children grew up with very happy memories of their childhood home. At the end of Springfield Passage was Springfield Cottage, a substantial detached house facing Gates' field. The cottages and Trinity Road itself were demolished in 1961, to make way for the flyover and roundabout linking Sish Lane with Lytton Way.

Almost next door to Holy Trinity, divided from it only by the Coach and Horses Inn, stands the High Street Methodist church. Methodism in Stevenage can be traced back to 1759, when John Wesley wrote in his diary for 2 August, 'At Stevenage we put up at the

Trinity Road, south side, 1963.

Gates' Slaughterhouse, Trinity Road, mid-twentieth century.

Holy Trinity church. On the right is the Coach and Horses public house, which housed Stevenage's first Co-operative Society shop, in the early twentieth century.

same inn with Mr Venn'. He records two more visits, in 1777 and 1788, and another in 1790, when he preached here, probably at the house of a Mrs Parker.

The first Methodist chapel was built in Stevenage in 1829 by a Miss Harvey, at number 38 High Street. On 21 October 1874 a public meeting was held in this building to discus the 'Proposed new Wesleyan Chapel and School Rooms at Stevenage.' Events thereafter moved rapidly. On 27 July 1876 the foundation stone was laid on the site of previous open-air services on the corner of Sish Lane and four months later, on 23 November 1876, the new chapel was opened. The total cost, including land and building, was £1389 8s 2d. The old building at number 38 was sold to a Mr Shelford, after which it was used successively as the town's assembly rooms, a penny bazaar, the North Metropolitan Electricity showrooms and currently as the Old Town Library.

CHAPTER THREE

OLD TOWN

From the Bowling Green to Whitney Wood

For over 800 years the Bowling Green at the fork of the Hitchin and North roads, was the place where Stevenage people gathered to hear proclamations, to celebrate, or to remember the dead. It was also used to play bowls, as Samuel Pepys did in 1664, one of several occasions when he visited Stevenage. Entertainment of another kind arrived in 1913, when the urban district council approved plans submitted by Messrs Shrouder and Matthews for the 'conversion of premises on the Bowling Green known as The Dovecot into a hall for use for cinematograph exhibitions.' This was the beginning of the Publix Cinema.

During the nineteenth and early twentieth centuries, several large houses, many with extensive grounds, were built along the west side of Hitchin Road. One such was Ingleside, owned in the 1920s and '30s by the Rose family, of Rose's Lime Juice. Ingleside Drive has been built on the site.

Whitney Wood in the nineteenth century was much larger than now, almost filling the triangle bounded by Hitchin Road, North Road and Corey's Mill Lane, with its apex at the Bowling Green. Apart from Whitney Field, bordered by the North Road, the whole of this space was covered with trees. The earliest known record of the name is from the thirteenth century when it is given as 'Wytehey'. In the next century it appears as 'Wyteneye' and as 'Whetneye' in 1370. The meaning is probably 'at the white enclosure'.

One infamous individual associated with Whitney Wood was the highwayman James Whitney. He is thought to have been born around 1660, possibly in the Stevenage district, but his antecedents are unknown and one suggestion is that he took his name from the wood as his was not a local surname. Stories of Whitney's exploits, embellished and romanticised, were widely circulated. In 1692 his career came to an end when he was incarcerated in the notorious Newgate Prison, near St Paul's in London. He was publicly executed on 1 February 1693 and the story goes that, while in prison, he wrote a ballad, which ends:

To villainy I was inclined
For which I now must die.

Above: Ingleside, Hitchin Road, 1908

Left: James Whitney.

The True Effigies of James Whitney the Notorious Highwayman

An engraving, supposedly of Whitney in his cell at Newgate, also survives. Whether either of these are authentic, or whether they were written and engraved later is a matter of opinion.

More respectable residents at Whitney Wood in the nineteenth century were the Barclay family. Dr Andrew Whyte Barclay, an eminent physician, was born at Dysart, Fife, in 1817 and studied medicine at the universities of Edinburgh and Cambridge, became physician at

Whitney Wood, Mary
Barclay (left) and Henry
Noble Barclay.

St George's Hospital, London, physician to the King's household, and author of respected
papers and books on medicine. On 10 November 1871, he signed a mortgage agreement
for £5,000 to enable him to purchase acres at Whitney Wood at Stevenage in the county
of Hertfordshire and to build a house there. The landowners at the time were the
Ecclesiastical Commissioners, who had responsibility for the former estates of the Bishop
of London.

The house was built but seems to have been used mainly as the family's country estate,
since they also had a London residence. For example, the census returns for 1881 show
that the Barclays were absent from Stevenage at that time, leaving servants William and
Susan Hitchcock and Susan Stocks, a laundry maid, to look after the house. However,
despite frequent absences, the Barclay family took a keen interest in the life of Stevenage
and were generous supporters of local charities, particularly the Stevenage National School
(St Nicholas' School) on Burymead and the fund for the enlargement of the new Holy
Trinity church. The Barclays' son, Henry, born in 1866, took part in local social events
such as the cricket match in 1881 when he scored 7 for Dr Dunn's team in the first
innings and was out for a duck in the second. The Barclays also had a second child, their
daughter Mary, who grew up to take a leading role in the affairs of Stevenage.

After the death of Dr Barclay in 1885, Mrs Barclay, her son Henry and daughter Mary
continued to live at Whitney Wood. Mrs Barclay died in 1915 and a large stone memorial
cross was later erected in her memory in St Nicholas' churchyard. Henry Noble Barclay JP,
died at Whitney Wood on 7 February 1939, leaving his sister Mary who remained there
until her own death in 1946. She is still remembered by older people for her 'ready and
willing aid for the poor and sick'. The Barclay name is now part of Stevenage history: as
well as the Andrew Whyte Barclay memorial window in Holy Trinity church, there is the
Barclay School in Walkern Road, opened in 1949; Barclay Crescent, off Sish Lane, built in

the 1950s, and the short-lived Mary Barclay Home for confused elderly people, a modern building in the grounds of Whitney Wood, opened in 1974.

Whitney Wood house itself became an old people's home after the death of Mary Barclay. For many years friends and supporters organized a popular annual fête, with a rose queen, to raise money for the home. It was closed by 1965, after which Whitney Drive and the Old Walled Garden were built in the grounds. The house is currently occupied by a department of the North Hertfordshire District Council but plans have been submitted to convert it into apartments.

Corey's Mill

Until the boundary changes following the designation of Stevenage New Town, Corey's Mill was in Graveley parish. It takes its name from Henry Korye, whose wife Anne was the widow of John Tattersall, the previous miller. In 1613 she was taken to court accused of having poisoned him, but no further information has survived and it is possible that the case may have been withdrawn. The post mill burned down in 1878, leaving a few cottages, the house called Corey's Mount and a beer house known first as the Harrow, then as the White Horse, now as the Mill, owned by the Beefeater chain.

In recent years a new housing development on the site has been given the name 'Tates Way', perpetuating a much-repeated error which supposes that the paper-maker John Tate had a mill here in the Middle Ages. He did not. His water mill was at Hertford. It would have been more appropriate to name the new road at Corey's Mill after John Tattersall.

Corey's Mill Lane would now be unrecognisable to Henry Korye, or indeed, to anyone who had been away from Stevenage for forty years. The hospital which now occupies the area was opened by Queen Elizabeth the Queen Mother in 1972. Correctly called the New Lister

New Lister Hospital, opened by the Queen Mother, 1972.

Hospital, it replaces the Lister Hospital in Hitchin, which was named after Joseph Lister (1827-1912), the founder of antiseptic surgery, who attended a Quaker school in Hitchin.

The Avenue, Burymead and North Road

The central section of the path linking the High Street with the parish church of St Nicholas was planted as an Avenue with limes and horse chestnuts in 1756, by Rector Nicholas Cholwell. It was extended to the High Street by John Bailey Denton in 1857 and the final stretch was paid for by the people of Stevenage to mark the jubilee of King George V and Queen Mary in 1935. The Avenue is one of the best-loved features of the town.

North Road, also known as Baldock Road, was lined in the early twentieth century with substantial houses, such as St Margaret's and Whitegates, the latter being the home of Commander Clive Pinsent, who was Clarence Elliott's business partner in the Six Hills Nursery. Some survive today. Number 1 North Road, owned by Mr W.E. Franklin, was surrounded by a large garden, with a dewpond made in the early twentieth century, and a field, known as Franklin's field, where the overflow from Stevenage fair used to be held. In the late 1950s the field was developed as Franklin's Road and Dewpond Close.

The Burymead, part of the manorial lands owned by the Bishop of London, was once an extensive meadow where cattle were grazed. It has also been home to at least two schools. In 1558, Thomas Alleyne, Rector of Stevenage made provision in his will for the founding of three grammar schools one of which, Alleyne's Grammar School, Stevenage,

Alleyne's Grammar School. H.P. Thorne, headmaster 1915-1945, is front centre, with his family.

The Avenue, early twentieth century.

though much enlarged, is still operating from its original site on the Burymead, although it is now a co-educational comprehensive, renamed the Thomas Alleyne School.

Nearby is the School House of the old St Nicholas' School, (known originally as the National School) opened in 1834 and closed in 1963 when the new St Nicholas' School building in Six Hills Way was completed. The old school building was demolished and a new vicarage for St Nicholas' church built at one end and, beside a new underpass, at the other end, a house for Eric Claxton, deputy engineer to the development corporation from 1949-63 and chief engineer from 1963-72. It was he who designed the cycle tracks that are such a feature of Stevenage.

The old St Nicholas' School, opened in 1834, was showing its age when the New Town development began. Filled to overflowing with evacuees during the Second World War, it was again inundated in 1946 with children from the Briar Patch Home in Letchworth, who were housed at the Grange after their own premises were burned down. Boys over seven years went to Letchmore Road School and some returned at age eleven to the Avenue, to become pupils at Alleyne's Grammar School. Girls stayed at St Nicholas' up to the school leaving age of fourteen or, if they passed the scholarship examination, went to Hitchin Girls Grammar School. There were no inside toilets at St Nicholas' School, only two rows of 'offices' as they were known, at the far end of the school grounds, quite a daunting distance, particularly for infants.

Understandably, educationalists and the Urban District Council saw an urgent need to modernise and improve the facilities. But how much had been achieved in the homely

Right: Headmistress Miss F. Lawrence with children at St Nicholas' School, Burymead, 21 July 1952.

Opposite: Headteacher's house and school bell-tower, all that remain of the old St Nicholas' School, Burymead.

buildings of the old school and how much was owed to the staff, particularly the last headmistress Miss Lawrence and her deputy Miss Ferguson.

In the 1950s the Urban District Council built at its northern end a new estate called Burymead, with access from North Road. A little further on is a milestone of the Biggleswade and Stevenage Turnpike Trust, with the information that it is thirty-two miles from London. On the corner of North Road and Rectory Lane is the Marquis of Granby public house, now known as the Granby. It is situated near the Stevenage Turnpike, set up by the trust, to ensure that travellers paid their tolls for using the road.

Rectory Lane and Chancellor's Road

Woodfield, Rectory Lane, although considerably altered over the centuries, is believed to have been the original Stevenage Parsonage or Rectory until it was replaced by a new Rectory, built around 1780, which is the house now known as the Priory. One well-known owner of Woodfield was Admiral Fellowes, a leading resident of Stevenage. After the death in 1888 of his first wife, Constance, he married a neighbour, Margaret (Daisy) Jowitt, one of Rector Jowitt's nine daughters, in 1889. She outlived him by many years and was long remembered in the town for her kindness and generosity. Woodfield Road was built in the garden of their old home and they are also remembered in the name Fellowes Way, in Broadwater.

White Gates, North Road.

The Revd William Jowitt and his wife, Louisa, lived at Stevenage Rectory from 1874 until his death in 1912. His successor, Canon Molony, decided to sell the Rectory, which was in need of expensive renovation, and build a new smaller one in the grounds. This was accomplished by 1919, the architect being Sir E. Newton. The old building was given the name of the Priory, as having a religious connotation, and sold as a private residence. When Stevenage was designated a New Town in 1946, one of the three leading opponents to it was Michael Tetley, then owner of the Priory. He and his family moved away shortly afterwards, having sold the property to the Development Corporation who used it to house senior staff including R.S. McDougall, chairman from 1957-1967 and Robert Slessor, chief solicitor from 1947-1973. When the Development Corporation was disbanded in 1980, the Priory was once again passed into private ownership, and divided into two dwellings.

As for Canon Molony's new rectory, it was sold by the Church of England following reorganisation of the ecclesiastical parishes of Stevenage and Shephall in 1960, and Chestnut Walk was built on the site.

The Jowitts' only son, William Allen Jowitt, born in 1885, was an outstanding scholar. After a brilliant legal career he took up politics, somewhat controversially changing his allegiance from Liberal to Labour in 1929, and was Attorney General from 1929-1932. In 1945, as Lord Chancellor, he undertook much of the legal work necessary in drafting the bill that became the 1946 Town and Country Planning Act by which Stevenage was

The former Roctory, built around 1780, as it was in the nineteenth century. Now known as the Priory.

designated Britain's first New Town. Created Earl Jowitt and Viscount Stevenage in 1951, he died on 16 August 1957 aged seventy-two. His birth is commemorated by a blue plaque on the wall of his childhood home in Rectory Lane and a tablet in St Nicholas' church.

Earl Jowitt is also remembered in the road named Chancellor's Road, which was begun in the 1960s and has since been extended by several off-shoot roads, including Daltry Road, named after B.H.R. Daltry JP; Thurlow Close, named after O.P. Thurlow, who, with his wife had drapery shops at numbers 73 and 42 High Street and in Queensway in the early days of the New Town centre. He was a member of the Stevenage Urban District Council for some years. Chouler Gardens is also named after a draper, Frank Chouler, and Underwood Road after the Underwood family who had a saddlery at number 56 High Street.

St Nicholas' church probably began life as a wooden building at the heart of the original Saxon village of Stigenace. Its flint tower was built in stages from about 1100 and the nave was built, rebuilt and enhanced between the thirteenth and the fifteenth centuries. In 1841 a new south porch and a south transept were added. Very little is known about St Nicholas, after whom the church is named. He lived in the fourth century and has been one of the most universally venerated saints, being patron of children, unmarried girls, merchants, pawnbrokers and apothecaries. Santa Claus, his name in the Dutch language, has become a synonym for the mythical figure of Father Christmas, who evolved from legends of the saint's patronage of children.

The Old Bury, c. 1980.

Next to the church stands the Old Bury, the ancient manor house of Stevenage, dating from the thirteenth century. A new Bury was built next to it in the late nineteenth century. In recent years the Bury has been converted into apartments and two houses, the Firs and the Oaks, built in the grounds. The term 'Bury' meaning 'manor house' is not unique to Hertfordshire, but it has been used more extensively here than in other counties.

Weston Road, Rooks Nest and Almond Hill

Weston Road leading, as its name implies, to the village of Weston, has in recent years been blocked off at the hamlet of Rooks Nest, creating a cul-de-sac at this point. Two farm houses dating from the seventeenth century, or earlier, stand side by side here, Lower Rooks Nest, now known as Rooks Nest Farm, and Upper Rooks Nest, previously known as Howards and now as Rooks Nest House. For nearly 300 years the latter was farmed by the Howard family, until they left in 1882 and the property was acquired by Col. Wilkinson of Chesfield Park. In March 1883, the future novelist, Edward Morgan Forster, aged four, was brought to live here by his widowed mother. They stayed for ten years, a period of immense influence on the boy who grew up to write *Howards End*. The novel draws heavily on his childhood memories and includes some of the people he knew, such as the Postons of Highfield, who were prototypes for his characters the Wilcoxes.

Rooks Nest House.

In 1914, following the death of her husband Charles, Clementine Poston brought her son Ralph and daughter Elizabeth to live at Rooks Nest House. Elizabeth became a musicologist and composer and had a distinguished career with the BBC. After she and Forster met during the Second World War he was a regular visitor to his old home until his death in 1970. Since 1960 the countryside around Rooks Nest has been known as the Forster Country and it is the subject of a vigorous campaign to preserve it for all time as open green space for future generations.

In 1885 Stevenage received its first piped water, from a borehole almost opposite Rooks Nest Farm and House. This supply was a great improvement on the previous source of public water; five wells in the streets. The site of the borehole is now a small playground for children.

To the east of Rooks Nest, served by Great Ashby Way, are the recent developments of Weston Heights and Great Ashby. The origin of the latter name is currently proving difficult to trace. The area is not part of Stevenage but in the parish of Graveley and administered by North Hertfordshire District Council.

Trafford Close, Trent Close and Headingley Close, named after cricket grounds whose names link with the cricketing theme on the far side of Grace Way, were built in 1971 on a large field known as Mill Field, part of the land of the lords of the manor of Stevenage. It was sold in 1952 by the Ecclesiastical Commissioners who had succeeded the Bishop of London as lord of the manor in 1868 and later sold again for development. For 500 years

Church corner, Rectory Lane.

or more, from around 1273, there had been a windmill for grinding corn on or near this field, which has also been known as Churchfield. There is evidence of a mill being replaced or rebuilt at least once during this period.

Almond Hill and Almonds Lane are unlikely to have any connection with nuts, but probably take their name from the family of Reginald Alman, which was referred to in a manorial record of around 1350. In 1780 Richard Cholwell, possibly a descendant of Rector Nicholas Cholwell was admitted by Court Baron to land here known as Aumons.

Providence Road was built on the site of an old chalk pit, where previously stood Chalkpit Cottage. It is an unfortunate choice of name, likely to be confused with Providence Row, the cottages in the Cromwell grounds, which front on to Walkern Road.

Walkern Road and Church Lane

At the corner of Church Lane and Walkern Road there is an attractive group of cottages, several of which were built by Edward Vincent Methold, the Stevenage builder and local historian. He died on 31 March 1926, leaving four adult children. His wife had predeceased him. His distinctive 'EVM' emblem can be seen here and on other Old Town buildings. He was a dedicated local historian, who corresponded widely with others and was a member of the scholarly and highly respected East Hertfordshire Archaeological Society. In 1902 he published his *Notes on Stevenage*, the first separate history of Stevenage and the only one until Robert Trow-Smith's *History of Stevenage* was published in 1958.

Church Lane, c. 1914.

Church Lane from Walkern Road to Holy Trinity church was formerly known as Back Lane, providing access to the fields and smallholdings behind the High Street premises. It had also been known in the Middle Ages as Dead Lane or Dead Land and it was here that Rector Stephen Hellard established the charity to provide almshouses for three poor people. With others, he began to acquire land and a building as early as 1483 and by 1506, when he died, he left in his will, 'a messuage...newly built lying in a lane called Deadlane nigh unto Stanmer...which house I have built for the habitation of three poor folk without any rent wherefore to be paid so long as the said house doth or shall endure.'

After 600 years the almshouses, although rebuilt after the fire of 1807, are still fulfilling Stephen Hellard's will. 'Stanmer' was a farm, from which Stanmore Road, built in the Edwardian era, 1901–1910, takes its name. In 1835 the Stevenage Vestry built a fire engine house attached to the almshouses. When this was no longer needed the building was converted to a public bathhouse, run by the Urban District Council.

Basil's Road was built in stages from 1901, to house employees of the Eduction Supply Association and was reputedly named after the son of its managing director, Walter Woolard. Much of the construction work was carried out by the long established firm of W. Austin & Sons, builders and undertakers, from their premises in Letchmore Road. The Basil's Road houses were designed by various architects, including Mr Allen, RIBA, of Stevenage. An example of one of his designs shows the cottage with downstairs water closets linked to the main sewer, and to a piped water supply. However, collecting rainwater was still important and each cottage had its own traditional water butt fed by a

Fire Station, Basil's Road, 1961

down pipe, at the rear of the house for watering garden flowers and vegetables. Austin's also built the new fire station and a Roman Catholic Presbytery backing on to the Church of the Transfiguration in Grove Road.

The former Back Lane section of Church Lane was considerably widened in the 1960s but until then it had been no more than a rural lane, with hedges and fences enclosing fields between it and Letchmore Road. A blacksmith's forge stood in Shepherd's Yard and the 'spreading chestnut tree' still thrives on the site though now surrounded by the dwellings of Southend Close. Adjoining them, are the Inns Close almshouses, legacy of Jeremiah Inns.

The strip of land behind the fire station, reaching to Grove Road, which is now a car park, was the Urban District Council's yard until it moved to its current premises in London Road. During the Second World War the air raid warning siren was sited immediately behind the fire station. When the war ended it was kept in use for a time to summon auxiliary firemen, replacing the former fire bell.

Letchmore Road

By 1910 Hertfordshire County Council had commissioned a new school for boys in Letchmore Road. This was an elegant design, with the long windows and a little cupola in the roof that is so characteristic of Hertfordshire schools of that period. The building work

Letchmore Road.

Letchmore Road Boys School gardens.

was carried out by W. Austin & Sons and the school's capacity was for 332 boys. One feature was the school garden, in which the boys had individual plots and were taught horticulture, which was extremely important at a time when most people grew at least some of their own vegetables. The last headmaster, Mr. Roach, took over as head of the new Fairlands Junior School in Pound Avenue in 1951, and the Letchmore Road premises became an infants 'and nursery school.

Albert Street.

A short distance from the school, on the corner of Basil's Road, stood Coronation Cottages, named to mark the coronation of King Edward VII, which was planned for 1902, but had to be delayed because of the King's illness with appendicitis. The cottages were demolished by the Urban District Council in the 1960s, and replaced by a block of flats named Victoria Close, the name being suggested by the nearness of Albert Street. The latter road began to be developed in 1857 and was named after Queen Victoria's consort. In its heyday it housed a great variety of craftsmen and traders; cabinetmaker, photographer, hairdresser, fishmonger, hosier, dairyman, baker, umbrella-maker and many more, as well as two public houses and a Baptist church. By the 1960s the Urban District Council had decided that many premises in Albert Street were not up to modern standards and by 1964 demolition and redevelopment was taking place.

Letchmore Road is one of the oldest in Stevenage. It is mentioned in documents of 1451 and shown on a map of 1750. Letchmore Green, from which the road takes its name, was once considered to be apart from the town as a separate little community. In the nineteenth century the road near the green was crowded with the cottages of artisans and craftsmen, many of whom left here after the building of Albert Street and most of the remaining old cottages were demolished and replaced in the 1960s. However, the firm of W. Austin & Sons has been established there from around 1700 and the funeral directing part of the business continues to operate from these premises today.

At the lower end of Letchmore Road was Pound Farm which took its name from the Pound where stray animals were kept, or impounded, in more rural times. Until the late 1950s although the fields had been built over, the farm yard was still in operation, with a bull in his pen, next to a barn full of straw bales, with a pig-sty opposite, chickens running loose, and a cockerel crowing at dawn every morning. The farmhouse itself remained until the 1980s when it was demolished and four houses built on the site.

Primrose Hill, Pound Avenue and Sish Lane

Just off Letchmore Road, between Pound Farmhouse and the Old Workhouse, was a small piece of land known for a time in the nineteenth century as Trafalgar Square. The 1871 census reveals that some twenty or more people lived here, whose names included Day, Gayler, Leggett and Grimes. Intriguingly, there was on census day that year a travelling theatre company staying here, presumably living in wagons or tents. They were George Morland, artist; his wife and son; Alfred Bishop, travelling artist; his wife and two sons, and William Wiggins, aged sixteen, whose occupation was watchman.

In the 1920s, Albert Candler, who ran a local coach service from Stevenage to Hitchin, rented space at Pound Farm to park his vehicles. He called his company North Star Coaches after the public house of that name at number 12 High Street, which closed down in 1920. The next development came in 1933, with the building of a large cinema, probably on the site of Trafalgar Square, by Aston Ayres, who called it the Astonia, after his own name.

Pound Avenue was built in stages over a number of years, beginning in 1939, when a new road was opened up between the Astonia Cinema and the North Star coach garage on land at Pound Farm. The landowner wanted it to be called Shaftesbury Avenue, presumably because of its proximity to Trafalgar Square, but the Urban District Council were unenthusiastic. The first private houses, numbers 1-13, 2-10 and 24 - 34 were completed by Picton, the Knebworth builders, just as the Second World War broke out in the autumn of 1939. Before they were all sold, the last few were requisitioned for some of the many soldiers billeted in the town.

The Stevenage Brook known locally as 'the Ditch' flowed in a deep channel beside the Astonia car park before being piped under the road. The small piece of ground on its other side was used as wartime allotments and there were more allotments between Pound Avenue and Haycroft Road and at Primrose Hill.

For some reason a gap was left where numbers 12-22 might have been and Mr A.G. Lines' cows grazed there until 1942, when a social club for Irish women war workers was built here, called the Lytton Club in acknowledgement of Stevenage's largest landowners, the Lytton family of Knebworth. This building became the first home of the Lytton Players, the town's leading amateur dramatic group, which began as the ESA concert party in the same year.

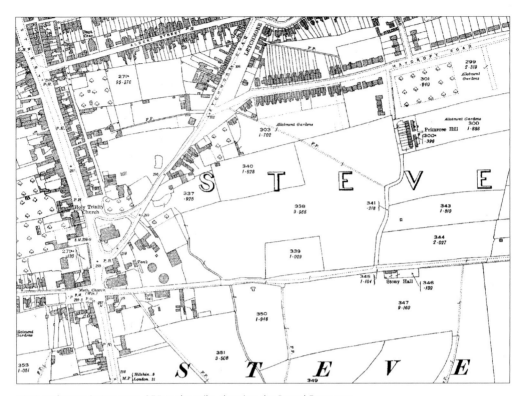

1881 Ordnance Survey map, 25″ to the mile, showing the Pound Farm area.

In the 1970s the building was used as an annexe of Stevenage College of Further Education until it was demolished and the site filled with houses and flats, some completing the missing numbers in Pound Avenue, others in Hammond Close, which took its name from John Hamond, barber and a citizen of London who bought land in Stevenage in around 1405.

Sish Lane has a long and well-documented history. It is associated with John Shish or Shush, one of the twelve jurors who gave evidence in the survey which was made in 1315 of land-holdings in Stevenage. Probably he took his name from Sishes, the place where he lived, as did the road leading to it. Today this runs from its junction with the High Street as far as Grace Way, but formerly for at least seven centuries it continued to Sishes End, near Pin Green. As the name suggests this road, although an important route to the town from outlying farms and cottages, was indeed a lane. It was narrow, bordered by hedges and grassy banks, with occasional cottages and openings for paths and field gates. Industry arrived in 1926 when the Pinkstone family opened the Stevenage Knitting Company in a former First World War army drill hall.

After the Second World War, to help cope with the post-war housing shortage, the Urban District Council erected some prefabricated houses (prefabs) in the field at the corner of Sish Lane and the path to Primrose Hill. These have since been replaced by the Sish Close houses.

Opening out from Sish Lane, the Urban District Council built several new roads in the 1950s and '60s. Barclay Crescent was named in memory of the Barclay family of Whitney Wood, Greydells Road is probably from a field name, Graveldell, and Langthorne Avenue is named in memory of Peter Langthorne, or Lankhorn, who held the office of constable in Stevenage in 1660. Ryecroft and Longcroft were also field names, mentioned in the 1315 Terrier (a survey of land), as was Haycroft, another road that was completed in several stages. On 26 May 1913 the Council minutes record the proposal 'that the 4th section of Haycroft Lane, having been completed to the satisfaction of the council's surveyor, be adopted under Section 19 of the Private Street Works Act, 1892, as a highway reparable by the inhabitants at large.'

Two roads built earlier in the century were named after local tradesmen and councillors: Ellis Avenue after draper and long-serving councillor, Thomas William Ellis, and Lawrance (sic) Avenue after Councillor Thomas Lawrance. Although the correct spelling is Lawrance, the road sign uses the more usual version. Ingelheim Court, off Hellards Road, is named after the town in Germany, with which Stevenage has been twinned since 1958.

Advertisement for the Stevenage Knitting Company.

Stevenage station, Julian's Road, early twentieth century.

The Railway and Surrounding Roads

In 1850 the Great Northern Railway opened a station at Stevenage, built on the site of Julian's, or Julliott's Farm, owned by Benjamin Hornett. As a direct result several new roads were built. Railway Street, linking the High Street to the station, was the first. Although its residents included several doctors and a veterinary surgeon, and the new town hall was built here in 1872, Railway Street acquired an unsavoury reputation and was partly redeveloped and re-named Orchard Road, after Orchard Court, home of John Bailey Denton. It was cut in half by the building of Lytton Way in 1976 and the remainder at the High Street end is now called James Way, after the jeweller's shop which previously stood on the corner at number 32, High Street.

Julian's Farm Road, now called Julian's Road, was built before the end of the nineteenth century and became known informally as Station Road, leading as it did from Hitchin Road to the station. It was built in stages, as was Essex Road, which began life as Percy Avenue, named after the son of Walter Woolard, managing director of the ESA, whose other son gave his name to Basil's Road.

It was the Great Northern Railway which built New Road in 1906 on land at Fairview Farm. However in the 1920s, at the request of residents, it was changed to Fairview Road.

Orchard Road, formerly Railway Street.

The Railway Inn (now The Mallard), Julian's Road.

Julian's Road, c. 1910.

High Street, Larkinson's shop can be seen on the far left.

In recent years it has been considerably filled in, and the fields and allotments between it and the railway line have been built over with new roads such as Hilton Close, which may or may not be associated with the name E.M. Forster gave to Stevenage in his novel *Howards End*. Larkinson, off Bridge Road, takes its name from the shop that sold household goods at number 41 High Street.

CHAPTER FOUR

SYMONDS GREEN AND FISHERS GREEN

Symonds Green and Woolenwick

Who Symon or Symond was and why a green should be named after him is an unsolved mystery. What is known, however, is that for many centuries the green had a completely different name and it is possible to state when the change took place.

William the Conqueror's Domesday Book of 1086 records that Robert Gernon held a small manor called Wluueneuuiche, where there was sufficient land for one plough team, meadow for half a plough team and enough woodland to support twenty pigs. The name appears again in various forms in medieval documents, for example as 'Wolwenwyk' in 1274 and 'Wolnewyk' in 1381. 'Wic' usually indicates a dairy farm, often in an outlying place. Thus, the probable meaning of the name is 'Farm of a woman named Wulfwynn'. By the twentieth century, all reference to 'Woolenwyk' seems to have ceased and the location of the Domesday farmstead to have been lost. The only link that remained was shown on the 1834 Tithe Map as two fields on the western boundary of Stevenage named 'Great Woolwicks' and 'Little Woolwicks', situated not far from the hamlet of Symonds Green.

There is now no doubt that the medieval manor of Woolenwick changed its name to Symonds Green during the first half of the seventeenth century. It has been possible to trace the change of name with some accuracy, thanks to the carefully preserved Stevenage Almshouse Charity Records, which date from 1483. The Hellard Almshouses in Church Lane depended for income on land held by their trustees and rented out to farmers. Most of the 'Almshouse Lands' as the fields were known, were in the Fishers Green area and their location is precisely described in the lease documents. In the will of John Huckle, in 1558 there is first reference to 'Symes Green'. A lease of 1605 reverts to the old name 'Wolwyck Green' and by 1668, a lease describes the land as Symonds Green, formerly known as Woolwick Green. There is a reference in the Hertfordshire Sessions' records for 1700 to a William Symonds and it has been suggested that he or his family may have owned, or been associated with, land at Symonds Green, but this will remain pure speculation unless more definite evidence is found.

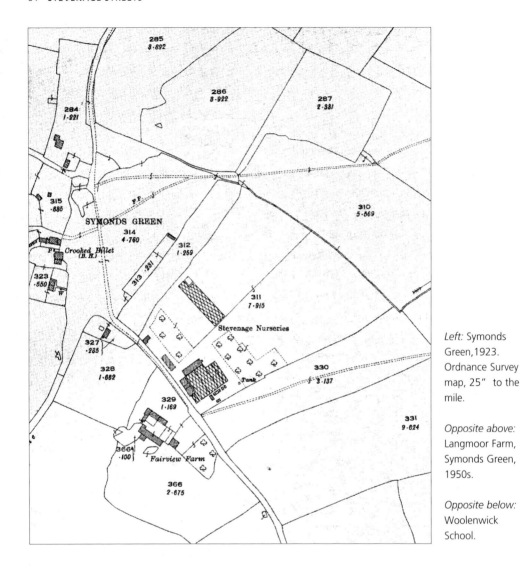

Left: Symonds Green, 1923. Ordnance Survey map, 25" to the mile.

Opposite above: Langmoor Farm, Symonds Green, 1950s.

Opposite below: Woolenwick School.

Meadowland

One important link between Symonds Green and the Woolenwick of Domesday was the existence of meadowland at both. Land of this type provided valuable grazing for animals and was usually near a source of water which encouraged the growth of lush grass. There were such meadows, until the late twentieth century, between Symonds Green and Fairview Road as indicated by the names Meadway and Oakmead. For the first half of the twentieth century the latter was the site of extensive nurseries, where flowers, fruit and vegetables were grown, both outdoors and in greenhouses. The Development Corporation's original intention, as set out in its 1949 booklet *The New Town of Stevenage* was to reserve the land west of the railway for industry and it declared that 'A number of

nursery gardens already established there will be retained and extended...No more houses will be built on this side of the railway...' However the 1966 master plan, prepared by the Development Corporation in accordance with instructions from the Ministry of Housing, proposed housing development at Symonds Green and by 1974 the first houses there were completed.

Today, Oakmead Nurseries and the surrounding meadowlands lie under the houses of Angotts Mead and the Meadway Technology Park. Woolenwick Junior and Infants' School, opened in 1973, keeps alive the ancient name for this place.

Until the developments of recent years, the hamlet of Symonds Green was reached by narrow lanes from Fisher's Green or Meadway, winding their way through fields and hedges, seemingly remote from the world. With its pub, the Crooked Billet, its pond, a few cottages and the donkeys tethered on the flowery mead opposite, the hamlet presented a picture of rural peace.

The Fox Twins

In the nineteenth century, most of the people living in the cottages worked on the land and times were hard for them when the weather was bad and crops failed. But straw-plait making provided a welcome additional source of income for women and children and sometimes for men as well. One who benefited from this skill in the 1850s was the wife of Henry Fox, a Baptist preacher who farmed ten acres at Symonds Green. He rented his cottage firstly from Sarah Moules, then from Thomas Franklin.

In 1857, Mrs Fox gave birth to twin boys in the same year as the opening of the Baptist chapel, or Ebenezer, in the newly built Albert Street in Stevenage. To mark this important coincidence, the devout Henry Fox called his sons Albert Ebenezer and Ebenezer Albert. The boys grew up to be poachers and their exploits became legendary. Their favourite ploy was to poach separately, making sure that one had an alibi. If the other was caught, he claimed mistaken identity and as the two were virtually indistinguishable, very often the case would be dismissed.

Some farmers regarded them almost with affection, turning a blind eye to their activities as long as they did not go too far. Others considered them scoundrels. They did earn a place in the history of crime, however, by taking part in the experiments on fingerprints which Sir Edward Henry was undertaking. Other people were also working on this, but his system was the one adopted. By using sets of identical twins, he was able to prove that every individual has a unique pattern of fingerprints, an invaluable weapon for the police and in 1901 a Fingerprint Bureau was set up at Scotland Yard.

Both twins died in Hitchin Workhouse, Ebenezer in 1926 and Albert in 1936. He was buried in St Nicholas' churchyard, at a funeral attended by the historian Reginald Hine and Lady Fellowes, widow of Admiral Fellowes, formerly of Woodfield, Rectory Lane. They laid a wreath of irises on the grave, together with this verse:

Gone to earth, old friend
And lost to mortal view.
Good luck to you where 'ere you wend,
Fresh woods and pastures new.

For many centuries there was a road from St Albans via Wheathampstead, Codicote and Langley through Symonds Green and Fishers Green to Corey's Mill and thence on to the crossroads at Baldock. This road had been important from Roman times and possibly even earlier, as a series of connecting prehistoric tracks. In the Middle Ages it was probably heavily used by pilgrims and traders on their way to the shrine of St Alban. In later

Above: Path from Fishers Green to Corey's Mill, 1904.

Right: The Fox twins.

centuries it began to diminish in importance as the main north-south road through Stevenage, which was to become the Great North Road, was increasingly used.

The Road from St Albans

One incident during the English Civil War sounds exciting today, but probably passed unnoticed by the cottagers in Symonds Green and Fishers Green at the time. The story is told by Alfred Kingston in his book on Hertfordshire during the Civil War. He describes how, in April 1646 King Charles I, having been trapped at Oxford where his army was besieged by Oliver Cromwell's Roundhead troops, managed to escape in disguise. Dressed as the servant of his own chaplain, he reached St Albans and spent the night of 27 April at Wheathampstead. The next day, travelling by the old road across country, he came through Symonds Green, Fishers Green and Corey's Mill on his way to Baldock, Royston and eventually to Downham in Norfolk. No doubt the details have been exaggerated over the years or perhaps it did not happen at all. Yet most stories contain an element of truth.

The old road still exists, now demoted to a sunken path under Clovelly Way, between Blakeney Road, Hopton Road and Grosvenor Court. It is cut off at its junction with Scarborough Avenue, then the route continues along Symonds Green Road to Fishers Green, then over the railway footbridge, continuing as Fishers Green Lane, across Ingleside Drive to Hitchin Road and Corey's Mill. Grosvenor Court is named after the Grosvenor family, Dr A.A. Grosvenor, his son, Dr Chetwynd and daughter Miss Dorothy Grosvenor who were prominent in the affairs of Stevenage.

Seaside Road Names

At the end of the nineteenth century many working class people lived in homes which were more like hovels, often built of wood, thus a fire hazard, or damp and certainly unsanitary by today's standards. Nor were there enough houses, even of this standard, given the increasing population.

Stevenage in 1901 had a population of 3,958, an increase of some 25% in twenty years. It is clear from census returns that at Fishers Green itself there were many overcrowded cottages. Conditions were made worse in around 1850 when large numbers of railway labourers came into the area. The arrival of the Educational Supply Association factory (ESA) in 1883 had given the town employment and also the opportunity to build brick houses for working people and so the group of roads nearby was built. Lymington, Bournemouth and Southsea roads, named after seaside towns, for whatever reason, were the originators of the seaside theme, later taken up for the Symonds Green development.

It has been suggested that Huntingdon Road may have been named in recognition of the fact that for several centuries Stevenage church government was within the Archdeaconry of Huntingdon, but this is by no means certain. Jubilee Road, however, was

Above: Bournemouth Road, 1950.

'New Town' post office, early twentieth century.

'New Town Rovers' Football Club, 1905.

so named in honour of Queen Victoria's golden jubilee in 1887, which was celebrated in great style in Stevenage. Collectively, this little group of roads became known as the 'New Town' and had their own football club, the New Town Rovers, and their own post office.

Scarborough Avenue

However, Scarborough Avenue, which is at the centre of the Symonds Green neighbourhood, has a name of more local origin. For the first half of the twentieth century, on the corner of Fishers Green Road and Nottingham Road stood Scarborough' grocery shop, which served the Fishers Green Community. It was run by Christopher Scarborough, until taken over by his daughters, one of whom, Miss Lilias Scarborough, was a much-loved and respected music teacher.

Nottingham Road was demolished when the Martin's Way viaduct over the railway line at Fishers Green Road was built in 1968.

When the Symonds Green neighbourhood was first built, a Co-operative store was opened in the small row of shops in Scarborough Avenue, but has since closed. Nearby is the Tom Tiddler public house, named after Charles Dickens' Christmas Story, *Tom Tiddler's*

The Tom Tiddler's Tavern, Symonds Green.

Ground, which is based on the tragic life of James Lucas, known as the Hermit of Redcoats, whom Dickens visited in 1861. Redcoats Green is a tiny hamlet on the road from Todds Green to St Ippolyts, just outside the Borough of Stevenage. Its name is probably derived from 'redcotes', meaning 'red cottages'.

Opposite the Tom Tiddler is the ecumenical Church of Christ the King, opened in 1982 and shared by the Roman Catholic, Church of England and United Reformed churches. Attached to it is a community hall and another hall and café, somewhat hidden, are sited in the former Co-op building. On the other side of Scarborough Avenue is Scarborough House, providing sheltered accommodation for disabled adults.

The name 'Fishers Green' is thought to be associated with John Fisher, who is mentioned in the Stevenage parish registers of 1643. It was also known as 'Hither' or 'Heather Green'. The first reference to the Fisherman beer house on the green occurred in 1897, although there was a beer house there from at least the 1830s. The present building dates from 1978, with later alterations.

The Educational Supply Association

Stevenage's first factory, the Educational Supply Association (ESA) had originated in Holborn Viaduct in London, where George Pannell Collings, a former headmaster who lived in Stevenage High Street, possibly at Springfield House, had begun a business to supply schools with stationery and other items. In 1868 he joined forces with another Holborn firm and together they formed Collings and Appleton at number 1, Grays Inn Road, London, with Collings as managing director and Appleton as chairman. Shortly afterwards they began to produce school furniture and registered the business as the Educational Supply Association Ltd. New premises were soon needed to allow the furniture department to expand and Collings was able to take over a small iron foundry which occupied an ideal site beside the Great Northern Railway in Stevenage. Here the ESA was able to innovate, introducing new school desks with cast iron legs, an advance on previous designs using oak or pitch pine. They went on in due course to introduce even lighter furniture.

The factory grew rapidly, becoming the town's major employer, and it was a disaster when, in 1907, a fire destroyed the buildings and their contents, including stocks of finished products and the workmen's tools, which they had to supply themselves. Two haystacks in a nearby field were also destroyed. The blaze was fought for over sixty hours by the Stevenage and Hitchin Fire Brigades. A relief fund, set up to help the men buy new tools raised almost £204, more than enough for the purpose, and the extra money was given to the Hitchin Hospital.

During the First World War fifty of the ESA's younger male employees joined the armed forces and a number of women were recruited in their place. In November 1918 a meeting took place in the town hall, in Orchard Road, at which they were urged to join the National Federation of Women Workers to protect their rights.

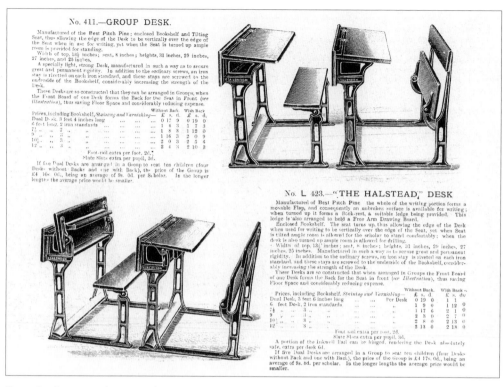

Illustration from an early ESA catalogue.

A second fire in 1938 destroyed most of the timber stock, creating such intense heat that it blistered the paint on Stevenage station and passing trains had to be sprayed with water. The premises were rebuilt with new timber sheds, drying kilns and a workers' canteen and continued to progress. A familiar sight, morning and evening, and at lunchtime, was the stream of workers cycling to and from the factory.

When the Second World War came, women again took the place of men who went to fight. The factory was converted to support the war effort by producing wings for Mosquito aircraft and over one million ammunition boxes. Where they faced the railway, the ESA buildings were disguised as row of cottages. A new timber store and a mill, with their own railway sidings, were built in 1942. In the Esavian building, units for the Mulberry harbours used in the D-Day invasions were made.

As normal production gradually resumed after the war, the ESA introduced innovations in design and production methods, such as the manufacture of beech-laminated desks and chairs. The firm also took over, or set up, other companies including those at Glasgow and Harlow and even designed and fitted out colleges in the Middle East. At its peak, the workforce was over 750 people. In 1976 a third disastrous fire occurred, causing over £1,000,000 of damage. Once again the factory was rebuilt with modern equipment

Julian's Road, workers going home from the ESA, 1957.

Stevenage station, with the ESA building in the background.

Holmsdale Terrace, Fishers Green Road.

including a metal finishing plant for powder coating metal furniture frames. But things did not go so well in the next few years and in 1983 the controversial publisher and industrialist Robert Maxwell took over the company, and four years later, it was shut down.

The ESA made a tremendous impact on Stevenage during its 100 years in the town. Until the new Gunnell's Wood Road Industrial Area was established in the 1950s and '60s, it was by far the largest employer in a town which was still largely agricultural. It even influenced the building of new houses.

It was in 1942, during the Second World War, that a small group of amateur singers and dancers formed themselves into the ESA Concert Party, beginning with three one-act plays and rapidly moving on to pantomimes and concerts, all produced by Fred Weiss, an Austrian refugee. As they became more ambitious, they found the stage in the ESA canteen too small so moved to the town hall in Orchard Road for some shows. They also began to entertain at the Lytton Club in Pound Avenue jointly with the Stevenage Entertainment Society. In 1948 the two groups merged, to form the Lytton Players, which became the leading amateur dramatic group in Stevenage, attracting membership and support from both old and new town people. It continues to flourish in its current headquarters, the Sishes, Vardon Road.

The closure of the ESA in the 1980s coincided with the privatisation of the railways and the government's decision to sell off land beside the tracks which had previously been used for such purposes as allotments for Stevenage. New roads built on the ESA site were named in the 'seaside towns' tradition for the area; Fleetwood Drive, Colwyn Close, Prestatyn Close, Morecambe Close, and Brixham Close, all adjacent to Torquay Crescent which had been built during the earlier development of Symonds Green neighbourhood.

CHAPTER FIVE

BEDWELL: SISH LANE TO WHOMERLEY WOOD

Stony Hall

Immediately to the south of Sish Lane, almost opposite the path from Primrose Hill, was a field named Stony Hall. It was mentioned as early as 1281, when it was 'le Stonhalle'. On the 1923 Ordnance Survey map two cottages are shown there, which local people remember as somewhat decrepit places of flint and brick, known as 'Six Bottles' because a row of bottle bases was embedded high up in one wall. At a meeting of the Urban District Council on 23 January 1939, the housing inspector submitted a 'report upon two cottages in Sish Lane known as Stoney [sic] Hall.' It recommended that as the cottages could not be made fit at a reasonable cost, proceedings be taken under the 1936 Housing Act to demolish them. This was resolved.

It was at Stony Hall in 1950, when Stevenage had been designated a New Town, that the Development Corporation began work on its first housing project known as the Stony

The start of the New Town, Sish Lane, c. 1950.

New estate, Sish Lane, c. 1951.

Hall scheme. Sish Lane itself had first to be widened and this work was carried out by the Urban District Council with financial help from the Development Corporation. The plan was then to build tall flats, shops and maisonettes on the Stony Hall site and some houses, or hostels in Sish Lane itself, to accommodate building workers. The difficulties and frustrations encountered by the Development Corporation at this time are described in Jack Balchin's book, *First New Town*. He also comments, 'Why the flats scheme was considered the right one for this site is difficult to understand. This was a rural town, to which tall flats were an unknown phenomenon. They were not even working-class flats as then viewed and they were to be positioned in a situation which would expose them to criticism as a monstrous outcrop.'

The Stony Hall buildings were largely complete by the summer of 1952. The first residents and many of their successors were mainly quite senior employees of the Development Corporation and professional people with jobs in the new industrial area. For example, the mother and sister of Robert Slessor, Chief Solicitor, lived there for many years until their deaths. Chauncy Road and Chauncy House, a six-storey block of flats, were named in honour of Sir Henry Chauncy, Hertfordshire's first county historian, whose *Historical Antiquities of Hertfordshire,* published in 1700, is still an invaluable source for local historians today. His family seat was at Ardeley Bury and as a boy he attended Alleyne's Grammar School in Stevenage from 1641 to 1646.

Local Notables

Of the other Stony Hall flats, Jowitt House is named after the Revd William Jowitt, Rector of Stevenage from 1874 to 1912 (see Chapter Two).

Bertram House is named after Julius Bertram who, in the early twentieth century, was MP for the Hitchin Division, which included Stevenage. A lawyer by profession, he was also a talented musician and a patron of the arts. At Sishes, his house in Pin Green, he entertained some of the leading writers, musicians and artists of the day. He was also very much against allowing women the vote and expended much energy in opposing suffragettes, including Lady Constance Lytton, of Knebworth. In parliament, he managed to prevent the 1906 Suffrage Bill from becoming law.

Bates House commemorates the sculptor Harry Bates, son of the Stevenage builder Joseph Bates. Born in 1850, Harry became a pupil at Alleyne's Grammar School and was expected to go into the family firm, but after a two-year apprenticeship as a stone carver he went to the Lambeth School of Art and then took up sculpture, specializing in relief work. In 1883 he won a Royal Academy gold medal and a travelling scholarship which enabled him to study in Paris under the great sculptor, August Rodin. Bates became the leading English relief sculptor of his time. His work was exhibited regularly at the Royal Academy and often photographed to illustrate Latin and Greek textbooks and he received commissions for public statues and from wealthy private patrons. He was elected an associate of the Royal Academy in 1892.

The Popple Way shops opened in 1953. This road was named after James Marsden Popple, who was chairman of Urban District Council from 1938 to 1946. He is remembered as a kindly man and a generous benefactor to Stevenage. For example, to mark the royal silver jubilee in 1935, he gave land for playing fields to be added on to the existing cricket ground in London Road, to create the King George V Playing Fields. In the 1950s, in conjunction with the Stony Hall development, the Urban District Council further extended the King George V Park, as it is now known, as far as Popple Way and Fairlands Way. Because of its location, between the old town High Street and the New Town centre, it was chosen as the ideal site for the first Stevenage Day in 1959. This has become an annual occasion, when the many voluntary, social and charitable organisations of the town set up displays for the whole town to visit. King George Close takes its name from the nearby playing field.

The name Claymores appeared as the field-name 'Claymer' in a document of 1451. Another field, Stony Croft, is mentioned in a document of the late fourteenth century. Brox Dell is a derivation of the 1551 field-name 'Brokedell' or 'Brokdelle' probably meaning 'Badger Dell'. Trigg Terrace is named after the innkeeper Henry Trigg, whose coffin is still in the rafters of the barn behind the former Old Castle Inn, Middle Row (see Chapter Two).

Walter Bedwell, the Plash and the Lane

The Urban District Council's first entirely new neighbourhood, developed in 1952-53, takes its name from Bedwell, a marshy area fed by a spring or plash. It was formerly reached by a winding footpath from Sish Lane, through meadows and cornfields, or by car from the London Road and up through Bedwell Lane. The earliest known mention of this lane is in a document of 1541, although Bedwell itself is referred to in a thirteenth-century charter. Some time later, certainly by the nineteenth century, it became known first as 'Dead Boy Lane' and then as 'Dead Man's Lane'. The 1863 abstract of title for the Guild of Literature and Arts refers to 'a certain field or close of land then formerly known as 'Dead Boy Lane Close' and later as 'Dead Man's Lane Close'. In the 1923 25 inch Ordnance Survey map the name had reverted to Bedwell Lane.

The will of Walter Bedwell, who died in 1536, sheds a gloomy light on life at that time. His wife was already dead and he himself was 'sick in body and fearing death.' He had four children, two boys with the same name, John the elder and John the younger and two daughters, Alice and Katherine, who were entrusted in their father's will with the care of the other children. It is very probable that this was a plague time, as Walter was aware that his children too, might die 'as God forbid' before they reached maturity. On a brighter note, he gives colourful descriptions of the clothes he was bequeathing: to Alice, his wife's best gown, another gown of violet lined with black cotton and a painted cloth. To John

Left: Fields near Bedwell Lane, c. 1952.

Opposite: High Plash, Cutty's Lane, 1963.

Dylleye, possibly a relative, he gave 'my green coat, my best doublet, my black jacket and my best hose.'

All traces of Walter Bedwell's house have long since disappeared, as have the more modern houses that stood in Bedwell Lane. The house at the top of the lane, opposite the spring, was known as Bedwell Plash and was the home of Clarence and Phyllis Elliott from 1907 to 1946. There were other houses and the sheds and barns of Bedwell Farm along the lane and a stream – the Stevenage Brook – ran under a low hump-backed bridge further down.

In 1941, during the Second World War, W.H. Sanders set up a machine shop in some former cowsheds belonging to Bedwell Farm. Here ammunition parts, submarine parts and other items for the war effort were manufactured. The factory expanded rapidly and workers were recruited from the surrounding villages, as well as from Stevenage itself. Both men and women worked in shifts throughout the day and night and even soldiers who were billeted locally came to do part-time work. The firm moved from Bedwell Lane to premises in the new industrial area in 1954.

Today, all that remains of the old Bedwell is the town centre pond which is fed from the spring at Bedwell Plash. It is possible to trace the route of the upper part of the old lane, as it runs down from the pond towards the town centre. Here, the name Marshgate may help to perpetuate the memory of the marshy ground at Bedwell, then all trace of Bedwell Lane vanishes under Westgate and Swingate. Some modern names, such as Bedwell Rise and High Plash, serve as reminders of what was here before the 1950s.

de Homles and Monks

The old field path from Bedwell led, via the field known as Pancake Corner, to Humley (Whomerley) Wood. The correct pronunciation is 'Humly' and, as the English Place-Names Society points out, 'The modern form [Whomerley] is corrupt.' The name can be traced back to at least 1287, when it was 'Homele' and there are many later references to the de Homele family associated with the wood. The name means 'house in the clearing'. There are still, in the wood today, the remains of a medieval moated manor house or farmstead which may have been the home of Ivo de Homle, who is known to have held land in Stevenage in 1275, or Ralph de Homle, whose name appeared in a document of 1293. The new St Nicholas' School, replacing the old building on Burymead, was opened in Six Hills Way, on the edge of Whomerley Wood, in 1963.

In 1967 the Stevenage Woodlands Conservation Society was formed, to help preserve the plant, bird and animal life of the woods and to help others to understand and enjoy them. The society established a wildlife sanctuary based on the moat in Whomerley Wood, but is no longer active. The road name Homestead Moat, although a little way from the actual site, is a reminder of the ancient dwelling in the wood. Unfortunately, nearby Cleviscroft is an example of an old field name being given to a modern road that is nowhere near it. Clevis Croft or Glevis Croft, which is very well-documented in the Hellard Almshouse records, was a field in Fishers Green. Whomerley Road is named after the nearby Wood.

Monks Wood, although contiguous with Whomerley Wood, was part of the parish of Shephall, which had a history quite separate from that of Stevenage until 1946. The manor

Headmaster J. Arnold with children of St Nicholas' School, Six Hills Way, 24 October 1972.

Aerial view of Whomerley and Monks Wood, showing new road layouts, 1950.

of Shephall belonged to St Albans Abbey and it is believed that the name Monks Wood is associated with the monastery at St Albans. Abbots Grove is named after the wood of that name. It is believed to refer to the Abbots of Westminster Abbey who were the lords of the manor of Stevenage from 1062 to 1550.

It was in the Monks Wood area that some of the first Development Corporation houses were let in 1951 and the first shops opened in 1952. Rockingham Way recalls the Rockingham coach that used to travel the Great North Road and stop at Stevenage High Street. It was in this road that the New Town's first public house, was opened in 1953. The pub acquired its name as the result of a competition. Don Hills, then a young reporter for the *Hertfordshire Express* newspaper, suggested this, the brewers were agreeable and the paper ran the competition. It was won by local historian Harold Roberts, who lived in Sish Lane. His suggestion was the Twin Foxes and this was accepted. A similar successful competition was held for the second public house, with the resulting name the Gamekeeper.

Lytton Land

The reason for the name Rowland Road is uncertain. One suggestion is John Rowland, who was Rector of Stevenage from 1397, but he was not the first rector (that was Nicholas Fitz-Simon in 1213), nor is much known about him. More likely is Sir Rowland Lytton (1561-1615). As Lord Lieutenant of Hertfordshire and Essex he commanded the counties' forces at Tilbury in 1588, the year of the Spanish Armada.

His grandson, Sir Rowland (1651-1674), was Sheriff of Hertfordshire, an MP for the county and supported the parliamentarians Hampden and Pym who visited him at Knebworth in the English Civil War period.

Not far away is Bulwer Link which commemorates the nineteenth-century writer, landowner and friend of Charles Dickens, Sir Edward Bulwer Lytton, and possibly also his mother, the eccentric Elizabeth Bulwer-Lytton, who was herself a considerable landowner in Stevenage and Shephall.

Bowcock Walk is named after Richard Bowcocke, or Brecocke, the highly regarded innkeeper of the Swan Inn, in the High Street, who was mentioned in Samuel Pepys' Diary in 1667. Not far away is Whittington Lane, named after another Swan landlord, Richard Whittington, who later built Broadwater Farmhouse and retired there.

Denton Road is named after John Bailey Denton, assistant enclosure commissioner for Stevenage, who lived at Orchard Court and took a prominent part in the life of the town in Victorian times, as did Dr George Dunn, who founded a medical practice in Stevenage around 1850, was joined by his son Dr Philip Henry Dunn in about 1887 and possibly also by a second son, Dr Robert Dunn. They are remembered in the name Dunns' Close. Nearby Jennings Close was a field name.

Bedwell Neighbourhood
Centre, 1958.

Bedwell Crescent

Bedwell Crescent shops opened in 1955. The community centre and St Joseph's Roman Catholic church were both completed in 1957 and Bedwell Secondary School in 1965. In the early days of the New Town, the Church of England established a congregation at Bedwell, at first in temporary accommodation, then at the purpose-built St Andrew's church in Bedwell Crescent, between Priory Dell and Abbots Grove. Much was achieved here through the energetic leadership of the Revd. Edward Harper, who came to Stevenage initially as a curate in the parish of St Nicholas' with Holy Trinity, then became priest-in-charge of St Andrew's from 1952-1955.

After the completion of St George's church, the St Albans diocese decided to merge the two congregations and the St Andrew's building was deconsecrated and eventually demolished. Harper Court was built on the site, named after the Revd Edward Harper.

Trees and fields

Several roads near Whomerley and Monks woods have names associated with trees. These include the Lindens; Holly Copse; Elder Way, where the Mormon (Latter Day Saints) church, built by voluntary labour with help from overseas was completed in 1964; Buckthorn Avenue, where Shaftesbury Court, a six-storey block of flats for the elderly and five specially-designed bungalows for disabled people and their families was completed in 1970, and the Hawthorns. It is possible, though not certain, that Abinger Close is associated with Abinger Hammer in Surrey, one-time home of E.M. Forster. The scholarly definitive edition of his work is known as the Abinger edition.

Farm Close refers to the site of Broom Barns farm as does Broom Barns Junior and Infant School, opened in 1953 and Broom Walk. Vintners Avenue and Poppy Mead are derived from field names and Ruckles Close was 'Rokhulle' in the fourteenth century, probably meaning 'Rook Hill'. Colestrete and Madefeld were field-names of medieval origin as was Cutty's or Cutt's, a name which has also appeared elsewhere in Hertfordshire as the name of a farm.

A Congregational church hall opened in the modern Cutty's Lane in 1954 and the Friends' Meeting House in 1959. Keeping the connection, nearby Fox Road is named after George Fox (1624-1691) founder of the Society of Friends, and Penn Road after the Quaker William Penn (1644-1718) who founded Pennsylvania.

Silam Road is named after John Sylam, citizen and pewterer of London who owned four acres of property in Stevenage around the year 1405. A less fortunate man is remembered in Inskip Crescent. In 1656, certain of the inhabitants of Stevenage applied for a licence to allow them to collect money for Edward Inskypp 'who has suffered great want and poverty by a sudden and fearful fire which burnt his dwelling-house and stables down to the ground.'

CHAPTER SIX

THE NEW TOWN CENTRE

Danish Theme

The original town centre plan had a Danish theme, derived from its closeness to the Six Hills which, earlier in the century, had been thought to be the tombs of Danish warriors. As a result, a number of Victorian and Edwardian houses built near them along the London Road had been given names with a Danish flavour, such as 'Daneshill House'. There was also a record of an old road called 'Danestrete' and not far away was Gunnell's Wood, possibly once owned by a Danish woman named Gunnhilda. There is no surviving evidence of a Danish settlement at Stevenage, but the district was so close to the River Lea, the boundary of Danelaw, that it could well have been fought over and changed hands many times during the years of the Danish invasions.

Construction work on the New Town centre began in 1956, but the first phase was not completed until 1959. A new road called Danestrete, after the old track of that name, was built parallel to London Road, which at that time was the A1, the Great North Road, carrying an ever-increasing volume of traffic. Most of the houses lining the road, having been compulsorily purchased by the Development Corporation, were demolished, often after being used temporarily to accommodate workers from the new factories, or by government departments while they were waiting for their premises to be built. One such was Blackamoors a substantial house to the east of London Road built in a field of the same name.

Daneshill House was one of the first to go, but its name was retained for a new seven-storey office block, into which the corporation moved in 1961, transferring its staff from their previous premises at Aston House and number 13 Town Square. In the same year the Mecca Locarno dance hall opened a little further along Danestrete. In 1980, when the corporation was dissolved, the Stevenage Borough Council took over the new Daneshill House as its offices.

The name Danegate, although an entirely modern invention, continues the theme. New magistrates' courts opened here in 1975. On the corner of Town Square and Danestrete stands the Edward the Confessor public house, so named as a reminder that this king gave

Above: London Road, c. 1910.

Blackamoors.

An Advertisement for the The Locarno Ballroom from the *Pictorial Commemorative* newspaper, June 1967.

the manor of Stevenage to the Abbot of Westminster in 1062. The gift must have been confirmed by William the Conqueror, as Stevenage is listed in Domesday Book in 1086 as a possession of Westminster Abbey.

A second public house opened in 1966 on the corner of Southgate and St George's Way. Named the Long Ship, it used images of Danish warriors in a distinctive decorative frieze on its external east wall. This was destroyed when new owners made alterations to the premises in 2002.

Left: Advertisement for the Long Ship, 1967.

Below: Advertisement from *Hertfordshire Pictorial*, June 1967, celebrating Stevenage New Town's twenty-first birthday.

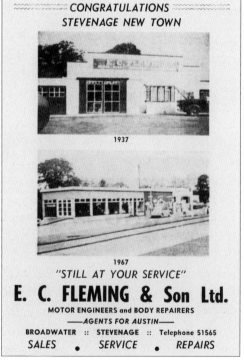

The King of Burundi visiting the
town centre, 14 December 1962.

Pedestrian Town Centre

Plans for the New Town centre did not come to fruition without delays and revisions. In
1949, at a public local Inquiry into the Development Corporation's Master Plan, there
were objections, from the Urban District Council and from the public as to the proposed
location of the Town Centre. These were overruled by the Minister of Town and Country
Planning, but there was a further, prolonged period of debate about the proposal for a
pedestrianised shopping area. This had first been put forward by Gordon Stephenson, the
Development Corporation's Chief Architect and Planner, in the 1946 draft Master Plan. It
was then considered a revolutionary idea, but when the views of the public were sought,
there was overwhelming support for it. Eventually, the architects managed to persuade the
minister to allow them to proceed with Britain's first pedestrianised town centre, which
was soon to attract visitors from all over the world. The first stage was completed in 1959
and Queen Elizabeth II came to Stevenage on 20 April that year, to declare the New
Town centre open. Queensway was so named in honour of her visit.

Above: Architects Vincent, Gorbing & Partners. From left to right: Leonard Vincent, Raymond Gorbing, Thomas Carter, Owen Roberts.

Left: 'Joyride' by Franta Belski.

In 1959 the Development Corporation transferred both its Estate Office and its Social Relations Department to number 13 Town Square. The former had previously operated in Stevenage High Street and the latter at Aston House.

Leonard Vincent was the Development Corporation's Chief Architect and Raymond Gorbing was appointed to lead a team to design and build the Town Centre. As a finishing touch the Czechoslovakian sculptor Franta Belski was commissioned to design a bronze statue entitled 'Joyride', sited on the platform in line with the clock tower. This was unveiled by Sir David Bowes Lyon, Lord Lieutenant of Hertfordshire, in 1958. It has appeared in countless photographs and has come to be recognised as a symbol of Stevenage. Belski was subsequently commissioned to create a memorial plaque to Lewis Silkin, 'Father of the New Towns' which was unveiled by the Rt Hon. Harold Wilson MP in 1974.

By naming the access road into the town centre as 'gates' – Eastgate, Swin[south-west]gate, Northgate, Marshgate, Westgate – the planners probably had in mind the old walled cities of the past, but here the Town Centre is defended with blocks of shops and offices rather than defensive walls. In Swingate, Brickdale House, an office block to accommodate the government departments of Health and Social Security, Employment and the Land Registry, opened in 1966. A six-storey extension for the Land Registry was built in 1974. The name 'Southgate' did cause some confusion in the early days, when some Stevenage mail ended up in Southgate, north London and vice-versa. It was in

First phase of the New Town centre, 1959.

Southgate, Stevenage, that several Hertfordshire County Council buildings were sited. The new divisional police station was opened there in 1960 and the central library, the health centre and hospital outpatients department in 1961. In 1964 the Urban District Council transferred its staff from the old Town Hall in Orchard Road to offices in Southgate House tower block.

In 1959 Stevenage market moved from the High Street to an outdoor site at Eastgate. When in 1973 Stevenage's first multi-storey car park opened in St George's Way, a new covered market with space for 119 stalls and a cafeteria was provided beneath it, with the name Market Place. Westgate was redeveloped in the late 1980s, after the New Towns Amendment Act of 1981 transferred the assets of development corporations to the Commission for New Towns, which was required to sell them to the highest bidder. Today, the majority of the town centre premises are privately owned, apart from Town Square and some local and central government buildings.

St George's Way

In 1956 the foundation stone of St George's church was laid by Queen Elizabeth the Queen Mother, who was again present when the completed building was consecrated by the Bishop of St Albans, the Rt Revd Michael Gresford Jones. St George's Way, taking its name from the church, was initially constructed as a single carriageway, but in 1972 it became a dual carriageway and two pedestrian underpasses opened beneath it, decorated with concrete murals by sculptor William Mitchell.

St George's church, 1964.

In 1973, the Manulife building, an insurance company headquarters, was erected next to St George's church. The design, a seven-storey office block, was not what the Development Corporation had hoped for. It dominated its immediate surroundings and obscured the outlook from the east window of the church. To compensate, the Development Corporation paid for a new stained-glass window to block the view of the Manulife building. The window was designed by Brian Thomas, on the theme 'The Christian Year' and made at Whitefriars Studio, Wealdstone. It is believed to be the largest stretch of stained glass, unbroken by stone or concrete mullions, erected in any English church since the Second World War. Ironically, at the end of the twentieth century the once state-of-the art Manulife building was unoccupied and a target for vandals. After much difficulty in tracing the owners, the Borough Council, in 2004 succeeded in attracting grants which will enable them to convert the site into accommodation for key workers.

In 1977 the undercroft of St George's church was leased to the Borough Council and converted to accommodate Stevenage Museum, whose temporary premises at Woodstone, a large house on the London Road, were about to be demolished. The museum had begun in 1954, at the White Cottage, also in London Road, and moved to Woodstone in 1968.

A number of other public buildings were sited in St George's Way. In 1961 the Stevenage fire station in Basil's Road was closed and a new fire and ambulance station opened here. It was later moved again, to Hitchin Road, on the site of the former Longfield School, although the St George's Way premises still remain for the time being. The town centre

Town centre pond, 1964.

Bowes-Lyon House and swimming pool, 1966.

gardens were completed in 1961 and the swimming pool was opened by the Urban District
Council in 1962. It was upgraded and modernised at the end of the twentieth century.
Bowes-Lyon House, a centre for young people, was opened in 1965. It was named after Sir
David Bowes-Lyon, who had been chairman of the Stevenage Youth Trust.

Economic pressure and government decisions sometimes conspired to prevent the
Development Corporation from carrying out its plans. This happened with St George's
Way. In an interview for the *North Herts. Gazette* newspaper on 17 June 1971, Leonard
Vincent, a former chief architect and planner, reflected on the twenty-fifth anniversary of
Stevenage New Town, 'I think the present line of St George's Way was a ghastly mistake.
In the original Master Plan it was shown on the east side of the Town Park, roughly along
the line of the present Silam Road and that would have meant that the whole of the
central area and the park would have been within the pedestrian precinct.'

With the completion of the southern section of Lytton Way, a new railway station was
opened in 1973 by MP Shirley Williams. The following year the police station was moved
yet again to new premises in Lytton Way, its fifth home since Stevenage first had a police
station. The first was in North Road, it then transferred to a building adjacent to the
Town Hall in Orchard Road in 1874, before moving to purpose-built premises in
Stanmore Road, then to Southgate in 1960 and finally to Lytton Way. The former station
in Southgate was then taken over by the Hertfordshire County Council Social Services
Department.

The second phase of Town Centre shops, including Littlewood's, opened in 1963,
followed by Sainsbury's supermarket and twenty-seven other new shops. Extensions to

Littlewood's, Boots and Woolworth's were under construction as the third phase of Town Centre development began in 1969. This phase was completed in 1970 and among the new shops opened were Marks & Spencer's and MacFisheries.

The Arts Are Not Forgotten

Once the major part of the Town Centre had been completed, work began on the final planned area, at Northgate. Its name, the Forum, is reminiscent of ancient Rome and was perhaps inspired by the recent finds of Roman coins at Chells. An abstract sculpture in fibreglass by Jose de Alberdi was unveiled here in 1972 by Nigel Abercrombie, chief adviser to the Arts Council. The Grampian Hotel, with 100 bedrooms and eight shop units beneath, was opened in the Forum in 1973. It has since changed to the Hertford Park Hotel. In 1973 Tesco opened a supermarket here and, with the beginning of a revival of interest in film, two EMI cinemas. As part of the Westgate development in the 1980s, Tesco moved to its present site, which has subsequently been redeveloped at the end of Westgate, near the Gordon Craig Theatre.

The long-awaited Arts and Leisure Centre, incorporating sports facilities, an art gallery and a 500-seat theatre, by Vincent, Gorbing and partners, was opened by the Borough Council in 1975. Since then, thousands of theatre-goers have been grateful to architect Raymond Gorbing for designing such unusually comfortable seating, where there is room

The Forum, Town Centre, May 1986.

The Gordon Craig Theatre with original orange panels, beside a remnant of London Road.

to stretch out the legs. The original external appearance of the building, with its orange fibre-glass panels, earned it the nickname of 'Ray's orange box.' Since then, and to the regret of some, it was refurbished in 1994 to a bland, white finish.

The theatre is named after Edward Gordon Craig, actor and theatre designer, who was born in Stevenage at number 23 Railway Street (now Orchard Road) in 1872, although his family left here when he was still a young child. He was the son of the famous actress Ellen Terry and the architect Edward William Godwin, and began his own theatrical career as an actor, working for eight years at the Lyceum Theatre under Henry Irving. He then took up stage design but, finding that his ideas of simplifying the sets and emphasizing the actors were not well-received in England, he moved to Europe. His work was acclaimed in Germany, Italy and Russia. In 1906 he settled in Italy, published the journal *The Mask* (1908-29) and founded a theatrical arts school in Florence.

Edward Gordon Craig exercised great influence over scenic design in both the USA and Great Britain. His published works include *On the Art of the Theatre* (1911), *Towards a New Theatre* (1913) and *Theatre Advancing* (1921). He died in 1966, never having visited the theatre named after him in the town of his birth.

CHAPTER SEVEN

BROADWATER

The Hundred Courts

Broadwater, never more than a hamlet at the crossroads, was for many centuries the administrative centre for this part of Hertfordshire and gave its name to the Broadwater Hundred. During the tenth century local government in England was reorganized by the Saxons. Each shire, or county, as they came to be called, was divided into 'hundreds' for administrative purposes. The origin of the term is not certain: it may have derived from the meeting of representatives from one hundred families or from an area of one hundred hides of land. Sir Henry Chauncy, writing before 1700, explained the purpose of the hundreds, 'When the Inhabitants of this Land...were so greedy of Spoil and Rapine that no person could travel in safety, King Alfred divided the counties into Hundreds, to secure his People from Outrages and Robberies'.

An officer known as the hundred reve or hundredary or centenary, acting on behalf of the king, was appointed for every hundred. The ceremony which took place when a new hundredary was chosen is graphically described by Chauncy:

> ...and all the elder Sort of People did meet together at the usual place in the Hundred, on a certain day appointed, when they expected him; and as he alighted from his Horse, they rose up and paid their Reverence to him; then he, setting his spear upright, received of them all a Covenant of Association...after this Manner; Everyone touched his Spear with their Lances, and by this Ceremony, they did Solemnly vow their Obedience to his Government...

Hundred Courts met monthly and were responsible for proving wills, dealing with criminal offences, determining title to land and levying taxes. They usually met at an open place, but one with some distinguishing feature such as a tree, boundary stone, or crossroads. The latter probably influenced the choice of Broadwater as the meeting place, and hence the name of the division of Hertfordshire known as the Broadwater Hundred. Its area of jurisdiction stretched north-south from Willian to Hatfield and east-west from Great Munden to Knebworth.

Although the meeting place was originally at Broadwater in later years the courts met from time to time at Stevenage, though their whereabouts are unknown. The hundred courts were in operation until the Local Government Act of 1894 which set up district councils as their successors, but even after that local directories and guide books continued to include them.

The Roebuck

For centuries Broadwater was little more than a place at the fork of the roads from London and Hertford to the north. The hundred courts must have made a dramatic impact on the empty landscape, as representatives arrived from villages and scattered settlements for the solemn business before them. It is feasible to suggest that the meeting took place at the road fork, where later an inn was built. The Roebuck Inn, as it is now called, was originally the Broadwater. The earliest known records date from 1691, in which year it was leased by Sir William Lytton to the current occupant, William Eaves. It was still known as the Broadwater in 1770 but the change of name to the Roebuck occurred before 1790.

During the coaching era of the eighteenth and nineteenth centuries, the Roebuck was in an excellent position to cater for travellers. Inevitably, where there were coaches there were highwaymen ready to rob them and stories of their exploits spread rapidly. It is difficult to distinguish truth from legend, but there have been persistent tales of the notorious Dick Turpin's association with the Roebuck. The historian W. Branch Johnson, writing in the 1957 edition of *The Little Guide to Hertfordshire*, says, 'It seems that in 1737 Dick Turpin hid in the Roebuck under an assumed name, before his final flight to Yorkshire, where he was captured'. Certainly the developers of modern Broadwater thought this worth commemorating and gave the names Turpin's Rise and The Chace to two of the roads near the Roebuck.

Branch Johnson also quotes from a description of Hertfordshire in 1598 by John Nordern, who said of the name 'Broadwater' that it is so called 'not of the continual water, for the place is commonly dry; but at great floods the fall of the land water maketh it a great sea.'

With the increase in horse-drawn travel that followed the turnpiking of roads in the eighteenth century, the service of a blacksmith was required and there grew up along the Hertford Road, on the corner of Broadwater Lane opposite the inn, a few cottages and a blacksmith's forge. In 1779 a survey was made of the Shephalbury estate for the joint owners, Miss Catherine Nodes, Mr and Mrs Jacques and Mr and Mrs Price. It recorded that the blacksmith's house, shop and mead occupied just over six acres.

With the coming of the railways, the Roebuck's fortunes declined sharply. In 1874, a report for the Knebworth estates stated, '...since the Great Northern Railway has been opened the trade has considerably decreased and the buildings have been allowed to get

Roebuck Inn, Blacksmith's forge on the left in Hertford Road, 1910.

into bad repair'. However the inn survived and with the coming of Stevenage New Town, it found itself again a hub of activity as the Broadwater neighbourhood was developed.

Richard Whittington

Further along the road to Stevenage, near the field named Roaring Meg, stood Broadwater House, now demolished, and on the opposite side, nearer the road fork, was Broadwater Farmhouse, built for Richard Whittington, the retired innkeeper from the Swan in Stevenage High Street. He rented a total of forty-one acres, three rods and eighteen perches from the Shephalbury estate in 1779, including Spring Field, which has given its name to Spring Drive, over half-a-mile from its true site near Monks Wood. The word 'spring' in this part of Hertfordshire usually means a small wood or copse. Mr Whittington also rented Milestone Close, a field of over seven acres, that was situated, as might have been expected, beside the Great North Road just beyond Roaring Meg. Its name has been used for the road called Milestone Close, some two miles away in the Poplars development.

Arthur Young, in his *General View of Agriculture in Hertfordshire* published in 1804, was full of praise for Mr Whittington's up-to-date methods, writing of his treatment of clay soil, 'Mr Whittington, an excellent and improving farmer, who holds a large farm in this parish, chalked about four years ago [1790] land in the neighbourhood...and part of it bore a most luxuriant and even crop of clover.'

In the late twentieth century, after standing empty for some years, Broadwater Farmhouse was restored and enlarged and is now used for commercial purposes. A modern restaurant nearby called the Old Forge is not on the site of the original forge on the Hertford Road, which closed in the 1960s. Today, from the Roebuck into Stevenage, the Great North Road, once so empty, is lined with large retail premises.

New Houses

Following the New Towns Act of 1946, Broadwater was included in the designated area for development. This gave the opportunity to end the centuries old division of the tiny hamlet into two halves: the Roebuck and the land and buildings on the west side of the Great North Road were in Knebworth parish, while those on the east and along the Hertford Road, were in Shephall parish.

In 1949 some of the first houses to be built in the early days of the development corporation were the four cottages in Shephall Lane, Broadwater. As the area was developed, new roads were built between the old Hertford Road and the new Broadhall Way which eventually superseded it. Traffic in the Hertford Road became very heavy and, after bitter arguments between those for and against, it was closed to through traffic in 1978.

Work began on the Roebuck, Longmeadow and Marymead housing areas in 1953. Initially local names were used for new roads at Broadwater. Lygrave was a wood and a field name, recorded in the 1840 Tithe Award; Sleapshyde may be derived from the Old English for 'wet or slippery place'; the name 'Marymead' is a corruption of 'mirey' or 'marshy'; an indication of the tendency for land to flood; Wychdell was mentioned in a charter of 1390 and may have meant 'wych-elm dell'.

Longmeadow School, 1950s.

Marymead, 1954.

Other roads were given names of people associated with the district: Fellowes Way after Admiral and Lady Fellowes, of Woodfield, Rectory Lane; Nodes Drive after the Nodes family who were lords of the manor of Shephall from 1542 to the end of the eighteenth century; and Goddard End, named after a twentieth century farmer of Shephalbury Farm. The existing South Lodge of the Shephalbury estate has given its name to Lodge Way; Enjakes Close is built on the site of a bungalow of that name and Nursery Close recalls Spencer's plant nursery which was here from the 1950s to 1973. Brook Drive refers to the Stevenage Brook which runs parallel to the Great North Road, although today it is mostly invisible, piped underground.

Stately Homes and Prime Ministers

Road themes in Broadwater include stately homes and castles such as Badminton, Balmoral, Berkeley, Blenheim, Burghley, Caernarvon, Kenilworth, Petworth, Stirling, Windsor, and Woburn. Tree names and woodland themes form another group and a third is named after prime ministers, including Asquith Court, after Herbert Asquith, 1st Earl of Oxford, 1852-1928, born in Morley, Yorkshire, Prime Minister from 1908-1916; Walpole Court, after Robert Walpole, 1st Earl of Oxford, 1676-1745, born at Houghton, Norfolk, regarded as the first British Prime Minister; and Blair Close, on the other side of the B197, named after Tony Blair, current Prime Minister from 1997.

CHAPTER EIGHT

SHEPHALL

A Place where Sheep are Pastured

For most of its recorded history, until the Reformation of the sixteenth century, Shephall belonged to St Alban's Abbey and for administrative purposes it was included in the Hundred of Cashio, which was centred on St Albans. Stevenage and the surrounding villages were within the Hundred of Broadwater, which had its meeting place less than a mile from Shephall village. An added anomaly was the fact that Broadwater village was partly within the parish of Shephall. Such are the quirks which make the study of local history so intriguing – and so frustrating.

Shephall village.

Shephall Lane, early twentieth century.

For many years there have been arguments as to the meaning of the name 'Shephall', some authorities suggesting 'ashtree slope' as an alternative, but it is now possible to be confident that the name means what it says, literally 'a corner of land where sheep are pastured.' Shephall adjoins Fairlands and the word 'fair' has been shown in a paper by the Revd H. Hall to derive from a Scandinavian word meaning 'sheep.' The road that leads to Shephall village from Hydean Way today is called Fair Lane.

Lords of the Manor

At the Dissolution of the Monasteries, Shephall was taken from the ownership of St Albans Abbey in 1542 and given by King Henry VIII to George Nodes, sergeant-at-arms and Master of the King's buckhounds. For the next 200 years the Nodes family were lords of the manor of Shephall, until the early nineteenth century when it was sold piecemeal to the Heathcote family. It then descended to Samuel Unwin who had inherited the estate through his mother and, wishing to keep her name alive, changed his to Samuel Heathcote Unwin Heathcote. It was his son, Unwin Unwin-Heathcote who, in 1864, demolished the old manor house and replaced it with the impressive neo-Gothic building by the eminent Victorian architect T. Roger Smith. This is the building which stands today. Shephalbury remained the property of the Heathcotes, although no member of the family lived there after the death of Colonel Heathcote in 1912.

Shephalbury.

Several roads in modern Shephall are named in memory of these former lords of the manor. The Nodes are commemorated in Nodes Drive, the Heathcote family in Unwin Place and Unwin Road and in Heathcote School, which was built as a secondary modern school in the early 1950s but used initially to house infant and junior children awaiting the completion of Peartree Spring Primary School, which opened in 1955. The Heathcotes are also associated with Wigram Way, which remembers the maiden name of two Heathcote brides, Eleanor Wigram, who married Samuel Heathcote Unwin Heathcote, and Frances Maria Wigram who married their son, Unwin Unwin-Heathcote.

The Polish School

In the 1920s the manor house was let to Mr David and Dame Maud Bevan and in the 1930s to Lt-Col. and Mrs Morgan-Grenville-Gavin. In 1939 it was sold to William Harriman Moss, who lived there with his family of five daughters. They shared the house during the Second World War with thirty-two children aged between two and five who had been evacuated from London by the Waifs and Strays Society. In 1947 Shephalbury was compulsorily purchased under the New Towns Act by Stevenage Development Corporation and soon afterwards it was let to Hertfordshire County Council as a school for Polish children.

An inspector who visited the school in 1953 commented 'It would be difficult to imagine a more delightful background for the education of these 32 girls and 523 boys...The house, with its lofty, sunny, rooms, makes a gracious setting for the family life that the headmaster and his four devoted staff have had the imagination and the sympathy to foster.' One of the four staff was Bernard Novak, a remarkable Polish man, who was a prisoner of war of the Germans, spent his time in the camp learning English and eventually came to Shephalbury to teach the children English. His book, *Thorns and Roses*, published in 1993, not only tells his own, very moving story, but also gives glimpses of life in Shephall during the early days of the New Town.

Meanwhile in 1958 a secondary school, rather confusingly also named Shephalbury, had been built in one corner of the Shephalbury grounds. The building was taken over by the Stevenage College of Further Education in the 1980s and later demolished. The private housing development there was given the name Grenville Road after the family who had lived briefly at the manor house.

When the Polish school was disbanded in the early 1960s, Shephalbury became home to another school, this time one for maladjusted boys, under the auspices of the Inner London Education Authority, but arrangements were made for the surrounding parkland to be open to the public. Then, in around 1991, the manor house was sold at auction and bought by the Coptic Church, leaving most of the grounds as a public park. Subsequently, in a joint operation between the borough council, North Herts. College and the Stevenage Football Club, a sports academy has been built in the field beside Broadhall Way.

Shephall Green

Before development, Shephall Green presented an attractive rural scene, with its church of St Mary dating back to the fourteenth century, its village pub, its trees, cottages and farm buildings. A lane ran from the Green round the outskirts of the grounds of Shephalbury and so by a winding route to the Hertford Road at Broadwater. Today this lane is a footpath. With the construction of Broadhall Way, Shephall was effectively divided into two, with the village on one side and the manor house and park on the other. An underpass beneath Broadhall Way provides pedestrian access. The village is equally constrained on its northern boundary by Hydean Way, which creates another boundary. Thus the old village green, designated a conservation area in 1974, is preserved almost as an historic relic, in isolation from its surroundings. However the number of new schools built on its periphery ensure that it does not rest in peace.

Records show that there was a public house on the green as least as far back as the early eighteenth century. The first known reference to the name is in a document of 1796, which records that Robert Smith gave up his tenancy of 'All that messuage or tenement on Shephall Green called or known by the name or sign of the Red Lion.' It is now called the Old Red Lion to distinguish it from the Red Lion in Stevenage High Street.

In years gone by an innkeeper or publican in such a small village as Shephall could not hope to make a living solely from this trade. Most also farmed the sixteen acres of arable land attached to the inn and some rented additional land as well. David Deards is recorded in the 1871 census as farming thirty acres. Others took up a second trade as Samuel

Shephall Green.

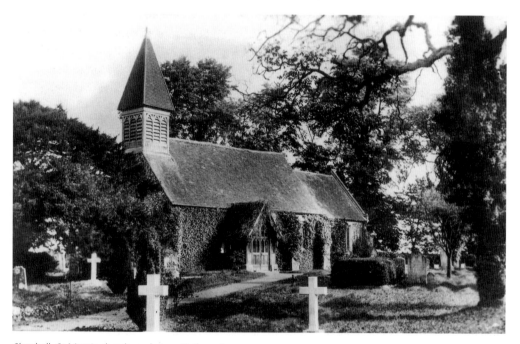

Shephall, St Mary's church, early twentieth century.

Carter, innkeeper and carpenter, was doing in 1861. Alfred Lake, who was innkeeper of the Red Lion for thirty years from the 1920s to the 1950s, used to keep pigs and farm several fields. The Old Red Lion was modernised in 1954 and subsequently considerably enlarged. It currently belongs to the Hungry Horse chain.

Shephall's ancient St Mary's church is Listed as Grade II and is notable for its medieval hammer-beam roof, its bell, the oldest in Hertfordshire at over 800 years old and an intriguing stone on the south wall of the chancel, which contains an inscription of possibly Saxon origin. The building also contains several monuments to the Nodes family, all by the eminent seventeenth-century stonemasons Thomas Stanton, his nephew William and great-nephew Edward. An interesting monument by Edward Marshall commemorates a previous vicar or the parish, John Rudd, who died in 1640. It was restored in the nineteenth century, with unfortunate results, as it now shows Mr Rudd with long grey hair. In fact the original has him carrying a lamb around his neck. Rudd Close, built in the 1950s, is named after him.

Church and Clergy

Several Shephall roads commemorate local clergy. Barnwell Road and Barnwell School, opened in 1960 as a secondary modern school, take their names from John Barnwell, rector from 1742-1760. Nearby Baddeley Close and Wortham Way take their names from George Baddeley, rector 1770-1792, and Walter Wortham, rector 1837-1877, while MacKenzie Square is named after Duncan Campbell Mackenzie, rector 1877-1892, and Warner's Close after William Warner, rector sometime between 1458 and 1539. Sisson Close and Leslie Close take their names from Thomas Sisson, rector 1792-1806 and his successor, The Hon. (later Sir) Henry Leslie, rector 1806-1837. Philip Godfrey, after whom Godfrey Close is named, was a curate at St Mary's church in 1822, but nothing further is known about him. Cholwell Road commemorates the distinguished Nicholas Cholwell, who was not only rector of Stevenage 1737-1773, and of Shephall 1760-1767, but was also the archdeacon of Huntingdon. Continuing the religious theme, Breakspear is a reminder that the only English pope, Nicholas Breakspear, was a Hertfordshire man, from Abbots Langley on the other side of the county, but in Cashio Hundred as was Shephall.

Shephalbury Estate

Many new roads were named after the fields on which they were built. A detailed estate map drawn up in 1779 shows all the fields in the Shephalbury estate and their tenants and is invaluable for historians. It was entitled *Plans of Sheephall Bury Estate in the Parishes of Sheephall, Stevenage, Aston and Datchworth in the county of Hertford. Belonging to Miss Catherine Nodes, Mr & Mrs Jacques, Mr & Mrs Price.* Some of the fields listed with this map have given their names to the new roads built on them. Randalls Hill was built over a nine acre field of the same name and belonged to Shephalbury Farm, which was leased to a Mr Matthews. He also rented Roaring Meg, a damp meadow next to a field called Little Sumps, a name also suggestive of marsh or swamp. This is not surprising, as both bordered the Great North Road at Broadwater, beside which ran the Stevenage Brook, which was liable to flood.

The name is not unique to Shephall, and is also found in other places, including at Hexton, in Hertfordshire. The English Place-Name Society suggest that 'roaring' describes the sound of a stream rushing over a bed of pebbles and 'Meg' refers to a noisy piece of ordnance. The Roaring Meg at Stevenage, currently a retail park, was for many years previously the town's sewage farm.

Old Names

Among other Shephall field names, Shackleton Spring gave its name to both Shackleton Spring and Shackledell. 'Shackle' was oak or beech mast, on which pigs fed, and 'spring' the local word for a small wood or copse. Peartree Way and the Peartree public house take their inspiration from Peartree Spring and it is thought that William Place is named for the variety of pear called 'William.' Before the new public house was opened, there was a competition run by the *Hertfordshire Express* newspaper to name it. The winner suggested 'The Partridge' from the Christmas carol *The Twelve Days of Christmas* but the brewers disagreed. However the modern inn-sign does feature a partridge in a pear tree.

Other wood names were Ridlins Wood, Loves Wood and the copse Leaves Spring, where development began on the road of that name in 1953. It made headlines in the February 1955 issue of the *Stevenage Echo,* the newspaper of the Stevenage Residents' Association, because of complaints of damp houses and delays in dealing with problems. Taywood Close is a modern invention, made up from the names of the builders, Taylor Woodrow. Cannix Close is named in memory of the manor of Cannix, sometimes spelled Cannocks, as in Cannocks Wood.

A number of roads, including Hydean Way, Hyde Green, Little Hyde, Long Hyde and The Hyde have names which are modern variants of Halfhyde, the farm which formed part of the Lytton estates. In medieval times a hide was a piece of land of variable measurement, sometimes reckoned at about 120 acres, but it was later used more generally to indicate an estate.

The Lyttons of Knebworth were, since the Middle Ages, major landowners in both Stevenage and Shephall. A letter survives, dated 30 June 1852, from Sir Edward Bulwer Lytton to his tenant at Half Hyde Farm. Having stated that there would be no increase in rent for the year, he added, 'you will kindly excuse me if I emphatically impress upon the attention of all that the above reduction can only be made upon the rents paid by the appointed day.'

Leaves Spring, 1950.

Ashtree School nature pond, Chertsey Rise, 1965.

Bandley Hill Farm Cottage, 1890.

When land was designated for the New Town in 1946, a major landowner in the Fairlands and Shephall area was Gonville and Caius College, Cambridge. In recognition of this, Gonville Crescent was so named. Bandley Hill was a farm, originally in Aston parish and the name may derive from 'Bandelvaley', which appears in a 1479 document with the possible meaning 'Beane Valley'.

Silkin Court was named after Lewis Silkin, the Minister of Town and Country Planning, who chose Stevenage to be the first New Town.

CHAPTER NINE

CHELLS

'A Very Difficult Name'

The name 'Chells', mentioned in Domesday Book as 'Escelvia' or 'Scelve', is thought to mean 'ash-tree slope' or possibly 'terrace of land.' By 1294, the family name of William de Chelsen was being used and there is a connection here with Chelsing near Bengeo, which the English Place-Names Society, in their volume *The Place-Names of Hertfordshire* sums up as being 'a very difficult name.' Sir Henry Chauncy, writing in 1700, spelled the name 'Cheles' and suggested, without foundation, that it was 'so termed from a Chil, a cold place'. It once shared a church with the tiny Domesday village of Box, but this was a complete ruin with only the foundations visible, by the time Chauncy's *Historical Antiquities of Hertfordshire* was published in 1700.

In 1086 land at Chells was shared between three of William the Conqueror's nobles, Robert Gernon, Geoffrey de Bec and the immensely rich and powerful Peter de Valognes. Its subsequent ownership is not easy to disentangle, but it is thought to have come into the hands of the le Strange and Pateshull families. However, Chauncy states that, sometime between 1216 and 1272, the manor of Chells was held by the Knights Templars and after them, the Knights Hospitallers, until Henry VIII's Dissolution of the Monasteries, after which it was held by John Norreys, who sold it in 1526 to Sir Philip Boteler and he, subsequently, to Sir Thomas Ashby who was holding it in 1727 and through him to William Hale of King's Walden and his descendants. The modern road names Knights Templars Green and Kings Walden Rise, built off the old Chells Lane, are reminders of the hamlet's history.

A Tiny Hamlet

Whatever its origin and early history, all available documentary evidence confirms that from 1086, when it was recorded in Domesday Book, until the late twentieth century, when it was developed as part of Stevenage New Town, Chells was never more than a tiny hamlet, closely associated with the woodland of Box and Walkern to the east, otherwise

Chells manor house, 1985.

surrounded by agricultural land. The manor house, a timber framed building dating from the seventeenth century, was considerably restored at the end of the nineteenth century and used as a farmhouse thereafter. Manor House Drive is named after it.

The hamlet's link with the outside world was Chells Lane, which led to the narrow, twisting road from Stevenage to Walkern. In the twentieth century, there were frequent complaints at Urban District Council meetings about the state of the Walkern Road at this point. On 31 May 1915 the council considered that the work by the Hertfordshire County Council of widening part of the Walkern Road near Chells Lane was unsatisfactory: it should have widened the metalled part! In due course the county's surveyor agreed. There was another problem on 30 April 1917, when the clerk was 'directed to call the attention of the district surveyor of the Hertfordshire County Council to the finger post near Chells Lane, the post having been knocked down'.

New Roads

When New Town development began in Chells, the first roads were given local field names, including Elm Green, where the first development corporation houses were occupied and shops completed in 1960; Collenswood Road and Collenswood School which was completed in 1963; and Mobbsbury Way, where the Nobel Technical Grammar School opened in 1962 and the Timebridge Youth and Community Centre in 1975.

Above: Stevenage Lodge, 1947.

Right: The Glebe estate office, Chells Way, 1959.

In Chells Way, St Hugh's church and the Swan public house opened in 1960. A swan was the symbol of St Hugh, hence the name. The ecclesiastical theme was continued by naming this part of Chells Way the Glebe, the medieval term for the land farmed by a rector. Chells Neighbourhood centre shops opened in 1963, the community hall and St John's Methodist church in 1964 and Ross Court opened in 1966.

Chells was one of the areas which presented the street-naming committee with problems because it ran out of field names for the many new roads being built. The help of two new grammar schools was enlisted. The Nobel School suggested names of scientists and engineers, while the Girls Grammar School chose names of famous women.

Roads named after Scientists, Engineers and Architects

Brunel Road Isambard Kingdom Brunel, 1806-1859, born in Portsmouth. This
pioneering engineer designed Clifton suspension bridge, built steamboats, including
The Great Eastern, his finest achievement. Chief engineer to the Great Western Railway,
1833-1846.

Darwin Road Charles Robert Darwin, 1809-1892, born in Shrewsbury. Buried at
Westminster Abbey. Voyage to South America and Pacific on HMS *Beagle* in 1831.
Published *On the Origin of Species* in 1859.

Edison Road Thomas Alva Edison, 1847-1931, born in Ohio, USA. His inventions
included the megaphone, gramophone, incandescent lamp, and systems of telegraphy.

Faraday Road Michael Faraday, 1791-1867, born at Newington, Southwark, London. A
physicist and chemist, he made many scientific discoveries, including the principle of
the dynamo. In 1829 he began a series of Christmas lectures at the Royal Institution,
primarily for young people, which continues to this day.

Harvey Road William Harvey, 1578-1657, born in Folkestone. Physician to James I and
Charles I. Discoverer of the circulation of the blood.

Nash Close John Nash, 1752-1835, born in London. Prominent in Regency architecture,
he had outstanding ability as a town planner, his designs included the layout of Regent's
Park and Regent's Street.

Nobel School Named after Alfred Bernhard Nobel, 1833-96, born in Stockholm,
Sweden. An engineer and chemist, he invented dynamite and left a large fortune in
trust for the award of five annual prizes for eminence in physics, chemistry, medicine,
literature and services to peace. The school opened in Mobbsbury Way in 1962 as a
new type of technical grammar school, aiming for the highest standards in both science
and the humanities.

Newton Road Sir Isaac Newton, 1642-1727, born near Grantham. English
mathematician and scientist who discovered gravity.

Telford Avenue Thomas Telford, 1757-1834, born at Westerkirk, Dumfriesshire. A civil
engineer, his work includes the Severn bridges, Ellesmere Canal, Caledonian Canal, and
St Katherine's Dock, London. He is buried in Westminster Abbey.

Wren Close Sir Christopher Wren, 1632-1723, born East Knoyle, Wiltshire. Scientist and
mathematician, he took up architecture in 1662 and was to rebuild St Paul's Cathedral
and fifty-two city churches after the Great Fire of London.

Roads named after Eminent Women

Anderson Road Elizabeth Garrett Anderson, 1836-1917, born in Aldeburgh, Suffolk.
Pioneer of the movement to include women in the medical profession. Lectured from
1875 to 1897 at the London School of Medicine for Women. Elected Mayor of
Aldeburgh 1908, the first woman mayor in England.

Nobel School, Chells Way.

Austen Paths Jane Austen, 1775-1817, born in Steventon, Hampshire, and died at
    Winchester. Her best-known novel, *Pride and Prejudice*, is partly set in Hertfordshire.
Aylward Drive Gladys Aylward, twentieth-century missionary to China. Biography *The
    Small Woman.*
Beale Close Dorothea Beale, 1831-1906. pioneer of higher education for women.
    Headmistress of Cheltenham Ladies College, 1858. Founded St Hilda's Hall, Oxford,
    1893.
Bernhardt Crescent Sarah Bernhardt, 1845-1923, born in Paris. Most famous actress of
    her day, she also managed several theatres. Toured in Europe, America, Australia and the
    Middle East.
Brittain Way Vera Mary Brittain, 1896-1970, born in Newcastle-under-Lyme. Writer.
    Books include *Testament of Youth*, about her experiences as a Red Cross nurse in the
    First World War. Married George Catlin in 1925. Mother of Shirley Williams, MP for
    Stevenage from 1964-1979.
Bronte Paths Sisters Charlotte, 1816-1855, author of *Jane Eyre,* Emily Jane, 1818-1848,
    author of *Wuthering Heights* and Anne, 1820-1849, author of *The Tenant of Wildfell Hall.*
Cavell Walk Edith Louisa Cavell, 1865-1915, born in Norfolk. Appointed Matron of
    Berkendael Medical Institute, Brussels, in 1907 and stayed after outbreak of the First
    World War. Court-martialled and shot for helping French, Belgian and British soldiers.

Du Pont factory, Wedgwood Way, Pin Green industrial area.

her last words were, 'Patriotism is not enough. I must have no hatred or bitterness towards anyone.'

Christie Road Dame Agatha Christie, 1891–1975, born in Torquay, Devon. Writer of detective stories, creator of detectives Hercule Poirot and Miss Marple.

Eliot Road George Eliot, pen-name of Mary Anne Evans, 1819–1880, born near Nuneaton, Warwickshire. Novelist, best works include *Adam Bede, The Mill on the Floss* and *Middlemarch*.

Fawcett Road Dame Millicent Garrett Fawcett, 1847–1930, born Aldeburgh, Suffolk. Social reformer and president of the National Union of Women's Suffrage Societies.

Ferrier Road Kathleen Ferrier, 1912–1953, born in Lancashire. Opera and concert singer. Successful tours of Europe and America. During the Second World War she sang for factory workers and the forces.

Fry Road Elizabeth Fry, 1780–1845, born in Norwich, the daughter of John Gurney, a Quaker. Married Joseph Fry, a Quaker banker in 1800. A prison reformer, she worked throughout her life to alleviate the dreadful conditions endured by women prisoners.

Nightingale Walk Florence Nightingale, 1820–1910, born in Florence, Italy. Reformer of hospital nursing. Took a party of thirty-eight nurses to Balaclava at start of the Crimean War in 1854. Became known as 'The lady of the lamp.' Awarded Order of Merit in 1907.

Pankhurst Crescent Emmeline Pankhurst, 1858–1928, born in Manchester. Formed Women's Social and Political Union in 1903 and devoted herself to cause of women's suffrage. Also her daughter, Dame Christabel Pankhurst, 1880–1958.

Siddons Road Mrs Sarah Siddons, 1755–1831, born in Brecon, Wales. Actress particularly known for tragic roles including Shakespeare's Lady Macbeth.

Other groups of roads were then 'themed', as follows:

Roads named after race-courses

Ascot Crescent; Ayr, Chepstow, Doncaster and Wetherby closes; Sefton, Lingfield and Sandown roads; Aintree and Derby ways.

Roads named after explorers

Cabot Close Sebastian Cabot, 1474-1557, born in Venice. Navigator, explorer and cartographer. Came to England after 1547 and subsequently opened up British trade with Russia.

Columbus Close Christopher Columbus, 1446-1506. Born near Genoa. Rediscovered America in 1492.

Cook Road Captain James Cook, 1728-1779, born in Marton, Yorkshire. Navigator, made voyages of discovery. Claimed Australia for Great Britain.

Drakes Drive Sir Francis Drake, c. 1543-1596. Born near Tavistock, Devon. Became the first Englishman to sail round the world. Played leading part in the defeat of the Spanish Armada in 1588. Newhaven, a Hertfordshire County Council old people's home was built in Drakes Drive in 1968.

Flinders Close Matthew Flinders, 1774-1814, born in Donington, Lincolnshire. Navigator, explorer and hydrographer. Explored Australian coast.

Frobisher Drive Sir Martin Frobisher, c. 1535-1594, born in Yorkshire. Navigator, Made voyages to Guinea, north Africa and North America. Frobisher Bay named after him.

Hudson Road Henry Hudson, d.1611. Navigator and explorer. little known about him, except for voyages 1607-1611. Hudson Bay, Hudson Strait and Hudson River named after him.

Livingstone Link David Livingstone, Scottish missionary and explorer, 1813-1873, born in Blantyre, Lanarkshire. Opened up central Africa to the influence of Christianity. Instrumental in abolishing the slave trade there.

Magellan Close Ferdinand Magellan, 1480-1521, born in Sabrosa. Portuguese navigator and first navigator of the Pacific Ocean. The Strait of Magellan is named after him.

Palmerston Court Quite why Palmerston Court is sited with the explorers is not clear. John Henry Temple, 3rd Viscount Palmerston, 1784-1865, was born near Romsey, Hampshire and was for many years a statesman and Prime Minister, so popular at one time that he was called 'Prime Minister for Life.'

Raleigh Crescent Sir Walter Raleigh, c. 1552-1618, born Budleigh, Devon. Soldier, explorer and poet.

Ross Court Sir James Clark Ross, 1800-1862 , born in London and his uncle, Sir John Ross,1777-1856, born at Inch, Wigtownshire, discovered the north magnetic pole.

Speke Close John Hanning Speke, 1827-1864. Born near Ilminster, Somerset. Explorer who discovered and named Lake Victoria.

Ross Court, Mobbsbury Way, 1960.

Stanley Road Sir Henry Morton Stanley, 1841-1904, born at Denbigh, North Wales. Went to the USA at the age of fifteen, later appointed correspondent for the *New York Herald*, sent to find David Livingstone in Africa in 1871 and greeted him with the words, 'Dr Livingstone, I presume!'

Roads named after Poets

Burns Close Robert Burns, 1859-1790, born Alloway, near Ayr was Scotland's greatest poet.

Byron Close George Gordon, 6th Baron Byron, 1788-1824, born in London, died at Missalonghi, Italy.

Dryden Crescent John Dryden, 1631-1700. Poet, dramatist and critic. Supported movement to make language clearer and more straightforward. Considered the foremost poet of his age.

Keats Close John Keats, 1795-1821, born in London, died in Rome aged twenty-six *Ode to Autumn* is one of his best known and enduring poems.

Marlowe Close Christopher Marlowe, 1564-1593, born in Canterbury. Dramatist and poet. Works include *Tamburlaine* and *Dr Faustus*. He had a formative influence on English contemporaries, including Shakespeare.

Shirley Close James Shirley, 1596-1666, born in London. Poet and playwright. Died in the Great Fire of London.

Roads named after Military and Naval Leaders

Barham Road Charles Middleton Barham, 1st Baron, 1726-1813, born at Leith, Scotland. First Lord of the Admiralty, 1805-6. Responsible for much reorganization of the British Navy.

Cromwell Road Oliver Cromwell, 1599-1658, born at Huntingdon. Leader of the Parliamentarians in the English Civil War. Signed the death warrant of Charles I. Lord Protector of England 1653-1658.

Marlborough Road John Churchill, 1t Duke, 1650-1722. Outstanding soldier. Commanded English forces in Holland against the French, in a series of great victories, beginning with the Battle of Blenheim in 1704.

Wellington Road Arthur Wellesley, 1st Duke, 1769-1852, born in Dublin. Soldier and statesman, most famous victory was the Battle of Waterloo in 1815, became Prime Minister in 1828.

Evidence of Romano-British settlement in the Chells area some 2,000 years ago was not discovered until recently. Apart from the Roman tumuli known as the Six Hills, and some evidence of road building, Roman finds in the Stevenage district had previously been comparatively few. In the 1980 the Chells Manor Village expansion of Stevenage was

Archaeologists at Boxfield Farm, 1986.

about to begin at Boxfield Farm, a site already designated an Area of Archaeological Significance. The developers, Hubert C. Leach and Moody Homes Ltd sought advice from Hertfordshire County Council's archaeological department, with the result that the Hertfordshire Archaeological Trust was commissioned to undertake a site evaluation.

Great was the excitement in 1986 when a hoard of 2,600 coins, mainly of the third century AD, was discovered in a broken pot in a shallow pit. The coin which provoked the most interest was one of the Emperor Pacatian, a little-known emperor who seized power for a few brief months in AD 249 and was then murdered by his own army. This was the first specimen of Pacatian's coinage to have been found in Britain.

Further excavations were carried out on the site and the remains of a Romano-British farmstead uncovered, with finds of pottery, Roman glass and metal objects. The archaeologists concluded that a disaster of some kind overtook the people of this settlement in the 370s, as their corn drier had been destroyed by fire and their pond and well were filled with domestic debris, including the remains of many cattle. So it remained, almost undisturbed through 1,600 years of farming until the upheaval of the 1980s. Most of the coins, glass and pottery are now in Stevenage Museum, with the remainder in the British Museum.

The archaeological discoveries provided interesting road names, mostly associated with the coins, the majority of which were minted between AD 200 and 300. They now present children in Chells with ready-made lessons in Roman history.

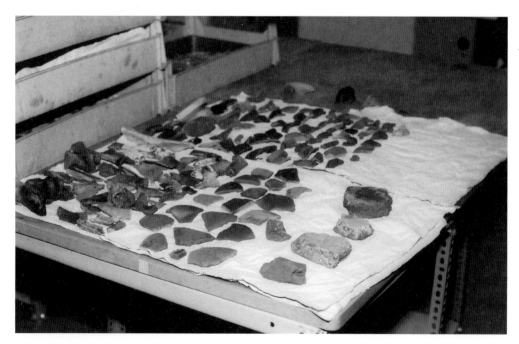

Pottery found at Boxfield Farm, 1986.

Roads named after people and places of ancient Rome

Emperor's Gate
Apollo Way Apollo was the son of Zeus and Leda in Greek classical mythology and
venerated by the Romans who built temples to him.
Augustus Gate The title 'Augustus' (venerable) was conferred on Gaius Octavius, first
Roman Emperor, 27 BC-AD 4 on 17 January 27 BC. All successive emperors were also
called Augustus.
Julia Gate Julia Mamaea, a member of the influential Julia Gens (family) was the mother
of Alexander Severus.
Valerian Way Publius Licinius Valerianus, died around AD 269. Roman Emperor AD
253-260
Trajan Gate Marcus Ulpius Trajanus AD 54-117, born in Italica near Seville, Spain.
Roman Emperor AD 98-117. Trajan's column in the Forum at Rome was erected to
commemorate his victories over the Dacians. However, the 52 Trajan coins in the
Chells hoard are from the time of Trajan Decius, AD 249-251.
Gordian Way Gordian III, Marcus Antonius Gordianus, AD 224-244. Known as
Gordianus Pius (The Good), he was proclaimed emperor by the praetorian guard in AD
238, at the age of thirteen and murdered by troops in 244.
Tacitus Close Publius Cornelius Tacitus, AD 55-120. Roman historian. His father-in-law,
Agricola, was Governor of Britain.
Alexander Gate Presumably not Alexander the Great, but Marcus Aurelius Severus
Alexander, AD 205-235, born in Phoenicia. Emperor from 222-235. The Chells coin
hoard contained 168 coins of his reign.
Fortuna Close Fortuna, Italian goddess of chance or fortune.
Hadrian's Walk Publius Aelius Hadrianus, AD 76-138, Roman Emperor 117-138, born
in Italica, Spain. Began building Hadrian's Wall between England and Scotland in 122.
Marcus Close Marcus Aurelius Antoninus, AD 121-180, born in Rome. Emperor 161-
180, author of a philosophic work, the *Meditations*.

CHAPTER TEN

Pin Green

The name Pin Green is thought to have come from the old English 'Pynd' meaning 'enclosure'. It was the home of Ralph la Pende in 1294. In the Stevenage Terrier of 1315, one of the jurors giving evidence was Roger Trot, who probably came from Trotts Hill at Pin Green, which was farmland until the New Town development began. A document dated Candlemass [Feb. 2], 1323/24 lists the measurements of arable land in Stevenage. It includes 'the land called John Gyles' which is probably the field listed in the 1836 Tithe Award as 'Giles Field'. In 1970 the Giles junior and infant schools were opened in Durham Road and named after the field. In the same year the Round Diamond School, also in Durham Road opened, named after a field called 'Round Diamonds' in the 1836 Tithe Awards, and located adjoining Martin's Wood.

Mossbury Farm is thought to have been associated with the family of John Morice, whose name appears in a document of 1294.

The name Sishes End is all that remains today of the large house and cottages that formerly stood on high ground at the end of Sish Lane. Documents of 1654 refer to 'a messuage called Shishes and meadow and wood belonging', but there are indications of even earlier origins. In a 1409 document 'Shusshgrene' is referred to and in 1451, Shussbys Land'. Census returns for 1881 state that the house was then in use as a cottage hospital for the town, although there were no occupants on the day the census form was completed.

In the early twentieth century Julius Bertram, MP, had lived at Sishes (see Chapter Four) When he left, it continued in private ownership until it came into the Development Corporation's hands. For fifteen years it was leased to Stevenage Youth Trust, a voluntary body supported by the Development Corporation and local authorities. In 1967, by licence from the trust to the Young Women's Christian Association, Sishes opened as a club and hostel for young people. In 1978, to the regret of all concerned, lack of money for upkeep forced the Development Corporation to demolish the house and use the site for building. The Lytton Players now have a centre there.

A similar fate befell Highfield, the substantial Victorian mansion off the Walkern Road, where in 1905 Elizabeth Poston, composer, was born. Her father, Charles, and his second

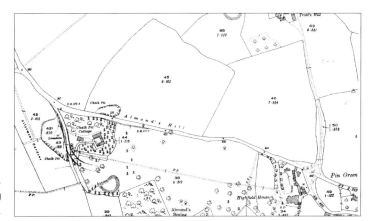

1924 Ordnance Survey map,
25″ to the mile, showing
Highfield and Trott's Hill.

Sishes. Demolished in 1978.

Below: Highfield House, 1914.

Highfield House, terrace and grounds, 1914.

wife, Clementine, Elizabeth's mother, were the inspiration for Charles and Ruth Wilcox, in E.M. Forster's *Howards End*. Charles Poston died in 1913 and his widow had to sell up and move to a smaller house, which she did the following year, taking her young son and daughter to live at Rooks Nest House on the Weston Road. Her daughter Elizabeth, who was born in 1905, became a composer and musicologist. She had a distinguished career with the BBC and was one of the panel of experts who helped to found the *Third Programme* (now Radio 3) after the Second World War. She was an authority on folk music and Christmas carols. Her enduringly popular carol *Jesus Christ the Apple Tree* is known throughout the world and usually included in the 'Nine Lessons and Carols' broadcast from Kings College, Cambridge, on Christmas Eve. But she was a prolific composer, a great deal of whose work is still unpublished.

Highfield Court, sheltered and warden controlled housing for elderly people was opened in 1969, a little way to the west of the old Highfield, but it does preserve the name. The memory is also preserved in the beautiful trees which Charles Poston planted in the grounds and which, with his other contributions to the Old Town, are his legacy to Stevenage.

Development of the Pin Green neighbourhood began near Fairlands in 1962 and the first shops and a community hall were opened here in 1965. With a few exceptions, most of the new roads in Pin Green have names which have no historic connection with Stevenage.

An early theme was famous sportsmen, including Archer Road, Lonsdale Road and Webb Rise, as well as:

Grace Way The major road dividing Pin Green from the Old Town, was named after the famous English cricketer William Gilbert Grace, 1848-1915. He was born at Downend, Near Bristol and his exceptional skill as an all-rounder earned him the title 'The Champion'.

Bradman Way Sir Donald Bradman was born in Cootamundra, New South Wales in 1908. He was a high-scoring batsman, knighted in 1949 for services to Australian cricket.

Douglas Drive J.W.H.T. Douglas, 1882-1930, an English cricketer who played for Essex and England.

Hendren Court 'Patsy' Hendren, 1889-1962, a cricketer who played for Middlesex and England.

Hobbs Court Sir Jack (John Berry) Hobbs, 1882-1963, was born at Cambridge. He was a highly successful English opening batsman, knighted in 1953.

Jardine Court Douglas Jardine, 1900-1947, a cricketer who played for Surrey and England.

Jessop Road Gilbert Jessop, 1874-1912, played cricket for Gloucestershire and England as an all-rounder.

Pollard Gardens The one road name which does have a local connection is named after Margery Pollard, a Stevenage lady whose family lived in London Road. In the 1930s she played for the Stevenage, Hertfordshire and England women's cricket teams.

Sutcliffe Close Herbert Sutcliffe, 1894-1978, born in Summerbridge, Yorkshire, was an English opening batsman.

Trumper Road Victor Thomas Trumper, 1877-1915, born in Sydney, New South Wales, an Australian cricketer.

Verity Way Hedley Verity was a Yorkshire and England cricketer.

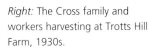

Right: The Cross family and workers harvesting at Trotts Hill Farm, 1930s.

Below: Aerial view, Trotts Hill, 1930s.

Wisden Road is named after John Wisden, 1826-1884, a sports outfitter and cricketer. In 1864 he published the first *Cricketers' Almanack*, containing detailed statistics and historical information relating to cricket. It has since been published annually and has become the cricket enthusiast's 'Bible.'

Bader Close, off Trumper Road, is unexpectedly positioned among the cricketers, but it does have a Stevenage connection in that it commemorates Group Captain Douglas Bader, the famous pilot of the Second World War who lost both his legs in action, and was briefly chairman of the Development Corporation from 1972-73.

Cricket grounds are remembered in Trafford, Trent and Headingley Closes on the west side of Grace Way and, in Pin Green itself, in the Oval, the main shopping and community centre. The first shops opened there in 1968 and the Pyramid Public House in 1973. The Development Corporation had originally hoped that, working in conjunction with the Hertfordshire County Council, the Urban District Council and local churches, it could provide, not only a community centre and more shops, but also offices, a library and an ecumenical church. Unfortunately, this did not come to fruition as planned and not until 1974 was it possible to open the building that housed the community centre and church. The latter was an ecumenical experiment, in that it was shared between the Church of England, the Roman Catholics and the Methodists. Before it was built the Church of England congregation in Pin Green met in temporary premises in two garages, calling themselves St Francis' church.

The new joint building was given the name of All Saints and was dedicated on 21 September 1974 in a ceremony conducted by the Bishop of St Albans, Robert Runcie (subsequently Archbishop of Canterbury), the Roman Catholic Archbishop of Westminster and the chairman of the London North West District of the Methodist Church. The community centre was opened earlier the same day by Dame Evelyn Denington, then Chairman of the Development Corporation. In 1975, Martin's House, named after the nearby wood, a specially designed home for the elderly, was opened for the Chauncy Housing Association at the Oval.

When Highfield House was demolished and the grounds turned into a public park it was given the name of Hampson Park, after Tom Hampson the British Olympic runner who won a gold medal for the 800 metres race at the 1932 Olympic Games at Los Angeles. He was Social Relations Officer of the Development Corporation from 1954-1965.

At the northern boundary of Hampson Park is the one great landmark of Pin Green. It's the water tower, 85ft high and visible for many miles around. It is sited at the highest point in Stevenage, 450ft above sea level. The tower holds 500,000 gallons of water, with an adjacent underground reservoir holding four million gallons.

In the early 1970s, land to the north of Martin's Way, which was confusingly given the name of St Nicholas, was developed very rapidly. The first houses in the St Nicholas area were completed at High Acres in 1969, beginning with Canterbury Way, where the St Nicholas shops, play centre and adjacent adventure playground were opened.

Perhaps in deference to the ancient parish church of St Nicholas from which it takes its name, this area of Pin Green consists largely of roads named after cathedral cities. Closest to home is St Albans Drive, but Canterbury Way, Lancaster Close, York Road, Durham Road, St Andrew's Drive, St David's, Manchester, Newcastle, Middlesborough, Winchester, Exeter, Southwark, Coventry, Norwich and Ely Close, Ripon, Salisbury, Lincoln, Chester, and Durham Roads all bear the names of cathedral cities, many of them linked by Pilgrims' Way as a reminder of the medieval practice of making religious pilgrimages to cathedrals and abbeys where the relics of saints were venerated. However there was also a street named Pilgrims in Stevenage in the fourteenth century, although its location is unknown. Constantine Close off Canterbury Way, is a reminder of the Roman Emperor Constantine I, AD 280-337, emperor from 306-337. His full name was Flavius Valerius Aurelius Constantinus, but he is referred to as Constantine the Great. By an edict of 313 he granted toleration to Christianity throughout the Empire.

Work began to develop the Pin Green Industrial Area in 1969 and in 1970 the first company, John Gibbons Ltd, moved in. Roads in this area mostly have names in memory of industrialists, including the following:

Boulton Road Matthew Boulton, 1728-1809, was born in Birmingham, and worked with James Watt on the development of steam engines.

Cartwright Road Edmund Cartwright, 1743-1823, probably born in Marnham, Nottinghamshire, where several generations of his family had lived.

Wedgwood Way Josiah Wedgwood, 1730-1795, born at Burslem, Staffordshire, potter.

Whitworth Road Sir Joseph Whitworth, 1803-1881, was born in Stockport, and has been heralded as the foremost machine - tool builder in the world.

At the end of Cartwright Road is Senate Place, which we might have expected to find with the other Roman names in Chells.

A quite different road name and again, having no connection with Stevenage, is Great Ashby Way, previously Islington Way. It leads to the very recent development of Great Ashby, which is currently outside the borough boundary and in the North Hertfordshire District.

The mystery of the name Great Ashby is at last explained. Apparently it is a name mde-up by the developers, who were impressed by the number of ash trees on the site. To 'ash' they added the suffix 'by' which is an Old Norse element meaning 'village' or 'settlement' (although not one that is usually found in Hertfordshire). The 'Great' comes from a modern document, for which the reference was not given, which refers to the building of new towns as 'the great extension'. Hence the new name, Great Ashby. Many thanks to Tony Evenden of North Herts. District Council for pursuing and solving this puzzle.

INDEX

Other local titles published by Tempus

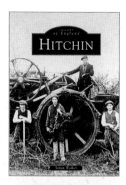

Hitchin
SIMON WALKER

Hitchin has seen a great deal of expansion over the last hundred years. Among the views of the town contained within this volume are those of the streets as they appeared as far back as 1860 and the cattle markets that once populated the town centre. It will provide a nostaligic look for all those who wish to know more about the heritage of this fascinating town.

0 7524 2937 X

The Witches of Hertfordshire
SIMON WALKER

This book examines the whole subject of magic, sorcery and the occult through the ages and includes discussion of phenomena such as cunning folk, werewolves, familiars and the archaeology of supersition and magic. Hertfordhire court records and a variety of accounts are examined to throw light on local witchcraft stories and other related incidents and dark doings.

0 7524 3203 6

Stevenage History & Guide
MARGARET ASHBY

The market town of Stevenage in Hertfordshire has long been considered an important location for travellers along the route from London to the North. This fascinating insight into Stevenage's past details the town's history from Saxon times to the present day and includes a walking tour of the town.

0 7524 2464 5

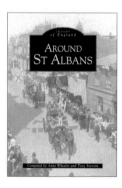

Around St Albans
ANNE WHEELER AND TONY STEVENS

This selection of images of St Albans and its environs are evocatively recreated using over 200 photographs, postcards and engravings, from the collections held by the St Ablans Museums Service. This book is a valuable pictorial record of this vibrant area which will delight all those who have visited the town and recreate the past for those who have lived there.

0 7524 2289 8

If you are interested in purchasing other books published by Tempus, or in case you have difficulty finding any Tempus books in your local bookshop, you can also place orders directly through our website

www.tempus-publishing.com